"Allen Nelson u
enlightens the new believer, encourages the mature Christian, and excites the theologian. The beauty of *From Death to Life* is found in its confidence in the sufficiency of the Gospel. It does not need our help; we need its power! Allen rightly contends that nothing is more inconsistent than proclamation with manipulation. His persistent, unrelenting insistence on the sufficiency of the Word of God preached in reliance on the Holy Spirit makes me yearn for my next opportunity to preach."

—Hershael W. York
The Southern Baptist Theological Seminary:
Victor & Louise Lester Professor of Preaching

"There is nothing in the world more important than the gospel of Jesus Christ. It is our primary message to be preached; it is the only message that saves. Over and over again, the Bible stresses the absolute necessity of getting this right, as well as the danger of getting it wrong. In his book, *From Death to Life*, Allen Nelson expresses and exposits the biblical gospel. With an earnest heart and ironclad conviction, he contends for the faith, refutes easy-believism, and takes his stand on the Word of God."

—Nate Pickowicz
Pastor of Harvest Bible Church in Gilmanton, NH
and author of *Reviving New England* and *Why We're Protestant*

"Allen Nelson calls us back to the true gospel in his book on salvation. His burden in this book is to see sinners who are truly saved by God's grace in Christ. If we go astray in our theology of conversion, then our churches may be filled with members who aren't truly believers, and both the church and the world suffer from the anemia present in such churches. Nelson explains what salvation truly is, reminding us that salvation is of the Lord. I gladly recommend this book for pastors and all who desire to understand the good news of Jesus Christ."

—Tom Schreiner
The Southern Baptist Theological Seminary: James Buchanan
Harrison Professor of New Testament Interpretation and
Professor of Biblical Theology

"*From Death to Life* is a beautiful, biblical explanation of what truly happens when a person is saved by the grace and mercy of our Lord Jesus Christ. The clarity of this writing can lead people to a much deeper understanding of what happens when this takes place in a believer's life, not only at the moment of conversion but also in the time following until the Lord calls us home. I pray this will be of great value as you seek a better understanding of this most important doctrine of salvation."

—Kallem Hill
Associate Pastor at First Baptist Church in Oppelo, AR

"Allen loves the gospel and the church, and he longs to see people truly converted to Christ. And yet his heart breaks for the many false converts who have been 'made' through unbiblical words and methods. In this book, he's not calling us to anything innovative—and that's exactly the point. I hear him pleading, 'Enough with the language and practices that have done so much damage and led to so little disciple-making!' He reminds us of what has always been and will always be God's way for someone to be saved. The result is a book that thoroughly explains the doctrine of salvation in words that are Scriptural and understandable (you'll love his illustrations!). I commend it strongly because if we embrace this book's tenets, we'll see people legitimately and lastingly converted to Jesus Christ."

—Steve Burchett
Assistant to the president, Christian Communicators
Worldwide, *www.ccwtoday.org*

"I've seen in Allen Nelson a passion for souls, which shows up in an intense desire to make Jesus Christ's saving message plainly known to everyone he can reach. *From Death to Life: How Salvation Works* makes every key gospel theme clear and, with God's blessing, will be a real eye-opener, not only to many who have not yet heard the gospel, but to a multitude of churchgoers who think they know it but have missed these indispensable root-of-the-matter issues. It's a book that will also greatly sharpen any new believer's grasp of our great salvation."

—Dennis Gundersen
Grace Bible Church, Tulsa, Oklahoma

FROM
DEATH
TO LIFE

FROM
DEATH
TO LIFE
HOW SALVATION WORKS

Allen S. Nelson IV

FREE GRACE PRESS

FROM DEATH TO LIFE:
How Salvation Works

Published by Free Grace Press
Conway, AR
freegracepress.com

Printed in the United States of America

Cover Design by
Stephen J. Melniszyn

ISBN: 978-1-59925-603-0

Dedicated to

Bradyn, Caleb, Ella, Piper, and Haddon

You are an undeserved gift to me and your mother.
I pray daily that you will know the God of your father,
and that He will move you from death to life.
Surrender your all to Christ the King. He is worthy.
I love you.

"Truly, truly, I say to you, whoever hears my word and believes him who sent me has eternal life. He does not come into judgment, but has passed from death to life."

John 5:24

Contents

Foreword

Sadly, too many people think salvation is obtained by a simple decision to "accept Jesus into one's heart." Salvation, they think, is secured by either praying the sinner's prayer, or by walking the aisle during the invitation. Assurance of salvation can be had, so they sadly think, once this decision is made.

Sadly, too many churches have little to no concern about false assurance. Once someone has made a decision to follow Jesus, the matter has been eternally settled. Thus, it is very rare for churches to urge their members to "make their calling and election sure"[1] and to prompt people "to work our their salvation with fear and trembling."[2] Churches are often afraid that such warnings could upset the congregation by undermining their assurance. Such promptings may even cause parents and grandparents to question the salvation of their wayward children and grand-children.

Sadly, too many professing Christians only want to be told nice things and be reassured of their salvation. When in doubt, reassurance can be had by looking back to the moment that they decided to give their lives to Christ and follow Him in baptism.

[1] 2 Peter 1:10
[2] Philippians 2:12

Sadly, too many people, too many churches, and too many professing Christians have a false assurance of salvation. Sadly, too many professing Christians don't know that they are unprepared to meet God.[3] They don't know they are in grave danger because they don't know what salvation is, what salvation does, and how salvation works. Sadly, their false understanding of salvation has lead to a false assurance of salvation.

Thankfully, Allen Nelson has provided a helpful corrective to a false understanding of salvation and to the false assurance that often follows. Thankfully, *false assurance* can be turned into *true assurance* for all those who have *true* faith in Christ Jesus and have a understanding of the *true* nature of salvation. Thankfully, *From Death to Life: How Salvation Works* does just that—it explains the true nature of salvation. Because this is a wonderful little book that every professing Christian needs to read, I am thankful for the opportunity and the privilege to recommend it to all.

—Jeffrey D. Johnson
Conway, AR

[3] Matthew 7:21

Preface

The greatest question in human existence is, *how can a person be made right with God?* The answer is not found anywhere else but the Word of God.[1]

The Word of God is our final authority on truth, for *all* of Scripture *is* truth.[2] Every word of the Bible is breathed out by God.[3] That is why you will see Scripture footnoted throughout this work. I implore you to look up the references, and carefully consider them. This work will be more meaningful when you do. Scripture is sufficient for these matters.

Any understanding of how salvation works that does not square with *all* of Scripture must be dismissed as insufficient. The Bible does not contradict itself.

As you will see, many in evangelicalism today have strayed from the truth of how salvation works resulting in dire consequences. In no way am I the infallible source of interpretation. My attempt has been to let the Bible speak for itself. Take up and read.

---

[1] Rob Bell once said, "the church will continue to be even more irrelevant when it quotes letters from 2,000 years ago." I reject that outright. The most relevant thing the church has are the very words of God. If we want the truth, we must go to the Bible.
https://www.huffingtonpost.com/2015/02/20/rob-bell-oprah-gay-marria ge_n_6723840.html
[2] John 17:17
[3] 2 Timothy 3:16, see *The Chicago Statement on Biblical Inerrancy.*

Twenty years from now you may have forgotten this book, but if the biblical principles we discuss within it stick, I'm fine with that. Eternal matters are at stake and the only sufficient, authoritative, inerrant, and infallible resource we have to understand them today is what the people of God have always had—the word of God. Please read this book with that in mind.

Sometimes I question my adequacy as a preacher, much less a writer. I've come to realize I couldn't do either without the grace of God, and the help of the faithful people He has given me.

Therefore, let me begin by expressing my gratefulness for the grace of God in Christ for my salvation. My salvation is all of grace, even if it took some time to understand some of the ramifications of this. And I'm still growing and learning by His continuing grace.

He has used an amazing number of people who've had a direct influence on this book. First of all, I thank my wife, Stephanie, for her patience and support in life, ministry, and in the time it's taken to write this book. She is a true gift of God and an encouragement to me beyond what I deserve. She has pushed me in this endeavor. She has kept the household in order and the children taken care of while dad spent extra time away completing this project.

Thanks to the church family of Perryville Second Baptist for allowing me to pastor them and giving me the time I needed to write. I love these saints and consider it a great joy and privilege to labor in the gospel alongside them.

Thanks to Jeff Johnson for his initial encouragement to write this book. A hearty thank you to Nate Pickowicz for his help in this project and willingness to kick me in the shins. You wouldn't be holding this book if not for his efforts. Kallem Hill and Eddie Ragsdale were the first two people to read this book and encourage me to publish it. They have been true friends to me over the years and I am blessed to have them in my life. Thanks also to Billy Crow, Amanda Geidl, Derek Vester, Carly Nalley, Kelly Tolley, Clif Johnson, Gunner and Liz Madewell, Sharon Wilson, Carolyn McCallister, Derek Melton, Drew Cox, Adam Willett, Danny Thursby, Richard Gambill, and others who read and/or offered feedback or encouragement for this book.

Thank you Stephen J. Melniszyn for your excellent work on the cover. Thanks Kelly Jones for being a great pastor and friend to me. Thanks to Mark Hargrove for helping sustain me during a difficult season of ministry where the seeds for this book were sown. Thanks to Prissy Wallace for her continued support of my ministry. She is one of the godliest people I know.

Thanks to Nathan Nalley for helping me wrestle through this issue better in 2011 and for being a faithful friend and encourager to me over the years.

Thanks to Brad Underwood and Phil Eddy for always reading my blog posts and telling me if I ever wrote a book that they'd read it (here's your chance).

Thank you, Deborah Howard, for your diligent editorial work on this project and going above and beyond in helping a rookie writer. This book is so much better because she took a chance on assisting a small-town pastor. She did a great job of ironing out my Arkansan so that you might actually understand what I wrote.

Thanks to my parents for your constant encouragement in all my endeavors. I probably shouldn't put anything in print without thanking Gene Tanner, who has been the single biggest flesh and blood influence on me in ministry. During the writing of this book a giant of the faith, R.C. Sproul, passed away. Praise be to God for his influence in my life.

Thanks to the other churches I have served and the men and women who have influenced me for the Kingdom.

So many others have poured into me in some way and are deserving of thanks. Your kindness to me has not gone unnoticed and God has been gracious to me through your influence.

May God receive the glory.

1

What Must I Do?

*"This is that which I seek for,
even to be rid of this heavy burden,
but get it off myself, I cannot."*
—John Bunyan[1]

Gripping the hilt with white knuckles, he momentarily pressed his sword to his own throat. Immediately, he felt the blade's dullness. He had neglected his weapon like he had neglected so many other crucial matters; but now there was no time left. It would all be over soon. He felt regret in every fiber of his being as his life was flashing before his eyes.

His life, like his sword, felt pointless. His military career did not turn out like he thought it would. Instead of fame and glory, the only permanent thing it left him was the grotesque scar just above his right eye. He was reduced to guarding inmates in the local jail. Wasn't there something more to life than this? Wasn't there something more to human existence?

With all that had gone wrong in his life, he felt the gods were out to get him. Surely, they laughed at his misery. How fitting

[1] John Bunyan, *The Pilgrim's Progress* (Philadelphia: B. and T. Kite, 1808), 17.

that an act of the gods, a great earthquake out of nowhere, would be the final catalyst for erasing his miserable existence. He could not bear the shame that would be brought upon his life because he had let the prisoners escape; nor could he stand to face the punishment that inevitably awaited him and his family for his stupidity. *How could he have fallen asleep so easily?* He squeezed his eyes shut and slowly pulled the sword away so that he could perform the final plunge to take his own life.

On the precipice of hell, the jailer prepared to execute the thrust that would end it all. Suddenly, an urgent, but compassionate voice rang out from inside one of the cells. "Do not harm yourself for we are all here!"

He couldn't be sure, but this sounded like the religious enthusiast they had brought in just yesterday. This rabble rouser stirred up the entire town with his unceasing gab about the Galilean who had supposedly risen from the dead. All this man, Paul, seemed to care about was a man named Jesus.

That's why he'd fallen asleep in the first place—that constant sound of Paul and his companion's singing. Not that the singing itself was anything extraordinary, but there was something genuine about it. Something pure.

Now the jail cell stood open, but the ones inside made no move to escape. *Why?* Lowering the sword, the jailer staggered toward Paul's cell. He called for a light as a million thoughts flooded his mind. Heart racing, he asked himself, " *Why would this prisoner care about his captor?"* The heavy, barred door stood wide open. *Escape!* And yet, he remained.

The sword clanged to the ground as the jailer entered the cell. His eyes fell on Paul and Silas. An unexpected fear and trembling seized his soul. At that moment, he knew the message he'd heard these men proclaim carried weight. He felt its heaviness on his heart. He realized, though they were in jail, he was the guilty one. Though they were in prison, he was the one in need of freedom. The One true God's judgment was undeniably coming but dare he entertain the thought of somehow escaping it? Could his sinful wreck of a life be salvageable?

The jailer fell at their feet. His trembling hands reached out to unshackle the chains keeping Paul and Silas bound together, which were fastened tightly around the prisoners' ankles only hours before. To his utter amazement, the bonds were just as unfastened as the cell door. He leapt to his feet staring intently at Paul and Silas, concluding this all was an act of this Jesus in who Paul had been proclaiming.

Why hadn't they run away? For the first time in his life, his angry mask slowly melted away. In his eyes were brokenness, shame, fear, and a faint sense of . . . what was it? The jailer realized it was something he'd never truly felt before—hope.

The irony of the situation was not lost on Paul. The miracle of their chains being unloosed paled in comparison to what Jesus was doing for this man. The silence continued until the jailer led them out of the cell and then slowly turned to face them again.

He didn't know what to do with his sin and shame. He didn't know how to fix all he had broken in his life. He bore a great burden that needed to be lifted but he didn't know how to remove it. But one thing he concluded: *these men had the answer.* He was willing to do whatever it took. And so, locking his eyes on Paul, he asked the question that would forever change his life: "Sirs, what must I do to be saved?"[2]

There is not a more important question anyone could ask than what that Philippian jailer did some 2,000 years ago. Unfortunately, a lot of confusion exists today about the right answer to that question. Ask fifteen people what it takes to be saved and it's not out of the realm of possibility that you'll get *twenty* different answers.

Christians in the 21st Century should be proficient in explaining what a person must do to be saved. We should be able to adequately answer questions like: How *does* one find salvation? How *does* someone move from *death* to *life*? How does salvation *work*?

Our standard thought should always be: *What does the Bible say?* This is our standard for truth, because what the Bible says, God says. Scripture is where we will find such answers.

Unapologetically, I assert that it is the Word of God that must shape our understanding of how a person becomes a Christian. After all, the Bible is our highest authority. This means when we want to understand how a person moves from

[2] While I've taken some liberty with Acts 16:25-30, I've sought to remain faithful to the sense and meaning of the text. True, we don't know the Jailer's background, and other thoughts may have raced through his mind. But the point remains, he was struck by these events in such a way that he wanted to know how to be saved.

death to life, we don't ultimately rely on tradition, experience, culture, personal testimony, or Oprah as our highest authority. It is Scripture that is wholly sufficient and authoritative to teach us the truth on this key matter. Here we stand!

What must a person do to be saved? A person is saved when the gospel is proclaimed and the Holy Spirit works through that proclamation in such a way that He moves the sinner from death to life, "turning on the light" so to speak. Only then can a person see his or her sin (the breaking of God's Law) and turn from it in repentance. Only then can they, by faith, trust in Christ alone as their only suitable and all sufficient Savior.

This definition of how salvation works flows directly from Scripture and also conforms to the faithful creeds and confessions of Christian orthodoxy throughout the history of the Christian Church.[3] If we adhered to a definition like this, perhaps we would see dramatic changes in the church today and in the lives of many people.[4]

We've traveled quite a journey to this critical epoch of evangelical history. Even now, many churches stand, though maybe unintentionally, with swords pressed to their own throats.

It is my hope that as we examine the reality of how sinners move from death to life that the light of truth will shine so brightly that all gimmickry and worldly entrapments will fall

---

[3] One particular confession we will examine is the Southern Baptist Convention's Baptist Faith and Message (2000) But you can also see: the Abstract of Principles (1858) article 8, the 1853 New Hampshire Confession articles 7 and 8, and the 1689 London Baptist Confession, Chapters 9-15.

[4] Certainly God is sovereign over salvation, but it's also gloriously true that He honors faithfulness to His gospel.

away. It is my prayer that you, dear Christian, will take these truths ever more seriously, so that God might effectively use you both in stemming the tide of false conversions in our day and in bringing lost persons around you from death to life.

May we be unashamedly dogmatic on how salvation works according to Scripture, all in an effort to see God work mightily for His own glory in our own hearts, local churches, and communities. The clock is ticking, but we haven't struck midnight yet. *Now* is the time to recover the answer to the crucial question, "what must I do to be saved?" *Now* is the time to be unmistakably clear on how salvation works.

2

The Walking Dead

*"Don't compare yourself to others
who call themselves Christians.
Compare yourself to Scripture."*
—Paul Washer[1]

"Dead men" live among us. Waiting in line for coffee. Cheering beside us at the ball game. Selling insurance. Liking our posts on social media. Eating at the corner table in the restaurant. Some are in the next pew over every Sunday. Some teach small groups and fill pulpits.

Perhaps one is reading this book.

And I'm not talk about a *physical* zombie apocalypse. I'm referring to the spiritually dead who walk among us.

There is a pandemic in America of false conversions to the Christian faith. Many people claim to be Christians who don't exactly fit the *biblical* definition of what a Christian is. They have a reputation for being alive, but are in fact dead.[2] This spiritual zombie apocalypse isn't coming. It's already gone viral and if the

[1] This comes from a sermon Paul Washer preached at the True Church Conference in 2007.
[2] Revelation 3:1

tide is not stemmed the church in America will fall mightily.[3] The alarm bells have been ringing for quite a while and we have no time left to hit snooze. It's time to wake up. The urgency for biblical fidelity has never been greater. Our opportunity is now.

Lest you think I'm suffering from Chicken Little syndrome,[4] in the state of Arkansas, where I live, over 75% of the population claim to be Christians.[5] I'm sure other states in the Bible Belt have similar stats, yet many churches are closing their doors as I write this, and numerous others are in the slow, agonizing process of dying.

Biblical Christianity and the local church are inseparable – you don't have one without the other. Unhealthy churches already show symptoms of the virus, and if they do not return to their first love, Christ, they will surely die of it.

Churches across denominational lines are beginning to recognize this sickness, and many are searching for a cure. It would be commendable to have both the zeal to diagnose the problem *and* implement the God honoring methods necessary to turn this trend around. Sadly, in too many situations, that is not the case. These churches don't always offer a *biblical* response.[6]

---

[3] Yes, we do have Matthew 16:18. But we must not think that this promise guarantees the church *in the United States* will forever endure. Jesus has the right to remove our lampstand (Revelation 2:5).

[4] You know: "The sky is falling!"

[5] http://www.pewforum.org/religious-landscape-study/state/arkansas/

[6] I am most certainly not indicting all churches here. Praise God for the countless churches seeking a biblical response. And for the ones who are not, may they see their errors and repent for the glory of King Jesus.

Instead they search for creative ways to entice people to come through the doors of a church building. *Whatever it takes.* If only they can get people to enjoy a worship experience, perhaps that person will eventually get around to loving Jesus one day.[7] The aim of this strategy is often to entertain, create a casual atmosphere, and make Christianity relevant.[8] Whether it's intentional or not, these aims too often result in a gospel message that is either watered down, or relegated to a minor part of the overall ministry.

Don't get me wrong, Jesus is still proclaimed from the pulpit, but He is no longer the primary attraction of the church.[9] Instead, it's a certain type of music, atmosphere, style of dress, or a specific subculture.[10] These churches have succumbed to the false belief that to fix the current crisis we need to just "get people in church." And in order to get them in church we need Christ *and* something else.

Sure, the Son of God taking on human flesh, living obediently before the Father, and dying a substitutionary death whereby He bore our sins that we might be brought into a saving

[7] In some cases, the *zeal* of these churches is commendable. They want to see people come to Christ. But their methodology is severely problematic in that it actually distorts the message of the gospel.

[8] Some of these aims are taken directly from church websites in my own home state. It is not my mission to attack a particular local church, but to make us aware of the danger of these sort of strategies. See another example in this article: https://reachrightstudios.com/make-churchs-technology-engaging-millennials/

[9] Sometimes Jesus is not actually proclaimed, or if He is, it's not the Jesus of Scripture.

[10] In particular, the 'affinity' based church plant movement has gained traction recently. These churches are often called 'cowboy church', 'biker church', 'outdoors church', and the list goes on and on.

relationship with the triune God is important, but fog machines are helpful, too.

Sadly, none of these attempts at new ways to get people in church address the root of the issue. The beautiful diamond of the gospel has been wrapped in toilet paper in the ridiculous attempt to make it more enticing. But as churches scramble for numbers, the deeper problem remains ignored.[11]

What's even worse is that these vain attempts at finding a way around Christ have almost inoculated people so as to prevent them from ever finding the real cure for their disease. Instead of improving the situation, our ingenuity has only worsened it.

The more pressing concern for why some people don't walk through the door of our churches has nothing to do with a service's ambience. It's the very same reason other people can sit in a church 52 Sundays a year and yet have no affection for Christ. These separate fruit issues share an identical root: *there is no spiritual life in many who claim to be Christians in America.*

Jesus said you *must* be born again.[12] That's the issue. This isn't just about getting people to come to church but about the devastating reality of the walking dead who are considered believers by themselves and others. These people have not passed from death to life. We won't correct this problem by trying to dress up the gospel any more than dangling a brownie in front of a dead man will make him hungry.

[11] See Jared Wilson, *Prodigal Church* (Wheaton, IL: Crossway, 2015).
[12] John 3:3

Consider Mike for example. Though completely fictitious, I bet Mike's just like a real person you know. He's living, breathing, walking, and moving, but he's not alive spiritually.

When he was 12-years old he repeated a prayer to be saved at Vacation Bible School per the prompting of a well-intentioned VBS instructor. Now that he's grown, he takes his family to church semi-regularly, puts money in the offering plate, and every now and then prays before meals—but not so much in public, of course.

What's the problem? There's no love for Christ in his heart.[13] There's no concern about the mission of Jesus.[14] The Bible is never meaningfully read or even considered except during the occasional sermon when Mike quits day dreaming long enough to pay attention.[15]

Although he is present at church a couple of times per month, it cannot be said that he truly loves God's people. He likes to arrive late and leave early so he doesn't have to hobnob with the other members. Sure, he *likes* most of them insofar as they are agreeable with him. But there's no eagerness to spend any real time with them, much less to lay down his life for them, to put their preferences above his own, to bear their burdens, or to serve them in any way.[16] Mike certainly has no desire to exhort

[13] 1 Peter 3:15
[14] 2 Corinthians 8:1-5
[15] Psalm 119:103
[16] 1 John 3:14, Philippians 2:1-4, Galatians 5:13, 1 Peter 4:9-11, etc.

his fellow church members to fight sin and walk in holiness.[17] *He* doesn't even do that.

This came to a head one night when his wife had the audacity to ask their Sunday school teacher to visit without consulting Mike first. Just as Mike feared, this Bible thumper found out some things he didn't want known and had the gall to suggest that Mike could not continue unrepentantly in his pornography addiction and still be considered a Christian.[18]

Mike fumed. It was none of that guy's business! And his wife should have kept her mouth shut! After all, *nobody* is perfect.

He paced across the floor, finally grabbed his Bible and showed this judgmental meddler the date he had written down 30 years ago. Case closed. He was a Christian because he had a date in his Bible.

Oh, what a tragedy to treat eternal matters with such frivolity. Mike would rather blame others than look at his own sins. Mike is a dead man walking, and if nothing changes, he will one day stand before Christ who will say to him, "Depart from me. I never knew you."[19]

A serious-minded reader of Scripture cannot help but observe that the current culture's definition of what constitutes a Christian, stands in stark contrast to the Bible's description of true believers – people who trust Christ, love Christ, follow

---

[17] Hebrews 3:14, Galatians 6:1
[18] 1 John 3:8
[19] Matthew 7:21-23

Christ, love Christ's Word, and love Christ's people. None of that is present in Mike's life.

The story of people like Mike resonates with most readers because we all have Mikes in our lives. From our perspective, they seem like "good" people.[20] Sometimes we conclude they are just immature Christians who never really grew in the years since their "conversion." The reality is, however, that they never genuinely came to Christ in the first place and stand in desperate need to be born again.

There's a chance that as I was describing Mike you had someone in mind. Mikes live in nearly every town in America, and are on the membership rolls of many churches.

In fact, it's even possible that a Mike is reading this book right now. If that's you, please understand that you are in a dangerous situation, but not a hopeless one. Keep on reading.

Why is This Happening?

Misdiagnosis can be fatal. Suppose you had an uncontrollable cough for months that just wouldn't go away. One day you actually coughed up blood. You decided a doctor's appointment was long overdue. When you arrive at the doctor's office, he looks you over for a few seconds, gives you a tiny sample of cough medicine and sends you on your way.

That is not a good doctor. He's given you a medicine that you don't need while leaving the serious problem you do have

[20] Although, in reality, no unbeliever does good. Not even one. Romans 3:10-12, Luke 18:19

unattended. If the true problem is never addressed you'll be dead in weeks. You can't fix cancer with cough medicine. Diagnosing the real problem is critical to curing it. You can't discover the solution to any issue until you accurately identify the problem.

Several streams feed into this river of evangelical deception, but a key contributor is a mistaken understanding of how a person actually becomes a Christian. One major factor in why we are so confused about how a person moves from death to life is the error of the Altar Call mentality and the Sinner's Prayer.[21]

Now I know many readers have been genuinely converted under such a system, and if you were, you're not the ones I'm talking about here.[22] The goal isn't to make you unnecessarily question your salvation, but to see the danger of this system we have created and even elevated to a *required* conclusion at the end of a church service.[23]

The Altar Call is the system of *coercing* sinners to the front of a church at the end of a sermon to elicit an immediate decision for Christ while a closing song is played. This deceptive system began in the early 19th century.[24] It often, though not

[21] See Appendices 1 and 2.

[22] The dangers of this system far outweigh any "benefits," but we are in such a results-based society that we want to see change *now.* Tradition in this system also keeps us from a willingness to let it go. My plea to you is to search the Scriptures.

[23] I hear men in my denomination regularly speak of the "necessity" of an Altar Call.

[24] See https://www.christianitytoday.com/history /2008/august/when-and-why-did-custom-of-conducting-altar-calls-begin. html

always, uses external methods to manipulate the hearts of sinners—things like the way the lighting is controlled or by employing emotive music or emotional stories. Anything that can be used can use to entice people to become Christians is considered fair play.[25] The ends justify the means. Sometimes the gospel presentation is deliberately so diluted that it's difficult to tell if a person is surrendering their life to the Lord of the universe or signing up to buy insurance from Him.

Most readers have probably experienced a service where heads were told to bow and eyes were told to close. "I see that hand!" Or, "We are going to play one more verse...This is your verse!" Maybe you've even been in a service where you were tempted to go up front just to so the pianist would not play the 18th stanza of *Just as I Am!*

Let me interject for a moment and mention that there are many faithful pastors in many faithful churches who use a system whereby people are *invited* (as opposed to coerced) upfront for further counsel at the end of a sermon and no manipulation is used.

It's basically something like "If you'd like to learn more about how to become a Christian, come talk with us." The idea here is that people would be given an opportunity to further discuss the things that they've heard during the sermon. This stands in contrast to the *Altar Call* mentality which (intentionally

---

[25] There have even been stories of 'planting' congregants who start coming forward so others will join them.

or unintentionally) manipulatively gears things toward a crescendo of responses at the end of a worship service.[26]

I am not questioning the motives of *everyone* involved in using the Altar Call. I have known and seen many faithful men who truly desire to see hearts change employ these tactics. Most of time, they simply don't know any other way to see people become Christians than the way they've always seen it done. Even if they may admit it is problematic, they are not really sure what else to do. This is the way it has always been done, so it's what we are stuck with even if statistics show the Altar Call is actually *counterproductive.*[27] What else can we do other than what everyone has always done?

Well, consider the fact that the Altar Call is actually the *new* approach.[28] For almost 2000 years of Christianity, millions of people were able to pass from death to life apart from such a misguided strategy. Jesus on the Mount[29] and Paul in the Areopagus[30] thought it sufficient to close their sermons without a synthesizer and drums.[31]

[26] I want to thank Hershael York for his input here and helping me not to lump everyone who uses some sort of invitation at the end of a service in the same category as those who pressurize people into making decisions.

[27] Some studies have shown as low as a 2-4% retention rate for those who come forward at an Altar Call. https://www.ccwtoday.org/2009/04/ the-corrupt-root-and-bitter-fruit-of-altar-call-evangelism/

[28] There is no evidence of an Altar Call used in Scripture or in Church History until the 19th century.

[29] Matthew 7:28 (See Matthew 5-7)

[30] Acts 17:32 (See v.22-31)

[31] Some make a "cultural" argument for Altar Calls, but how did this only become *necessary* in the last 150 years?

The Sinner's Prayer goes hand in hand with the Altar Call because, when a person comes up to the front of a church, he or she is frequently asked to repeat a prayer during this pressurized situation and voila – out comes a Christian. Again, I do think many know there is something off with this, but they are not sure what to do about it.[32] Nevertheless, what this entire system results in is something called *easy believism*. Jeffrey Johnson defines easy believism further:

> Easy-believism is the most widely accepted view of salvation, which is evidenced by the way most churches conduct themselves...Easy-believism is a watered-down view of salvation that comes from a low view of God and a high view of man. The notion is that [true] repentance is not necessary for salvation, and all that is required by God is a simple decision to 'accept Jesus into your heart'...With this low view of God, God does not demand any more from us than a simple prayer, which is often accomplished by repeating the words of the pastor after walking to the front of the church. At best, the preacher may remind us at the last second that we need to repeat the sinner's prayer from the 'heart.'[33]

In too many churches, we've essentially equated saying the right words to God as a third ordinance: Baptism, the Lord's Supper, and the Sinner's Prayer. Once this prayer is recited, it's

---

[32] I don't mean to say that we don't pray to become a Christian. I hope that's clear in the remainder of the book. Furthermore, "some people who have been led in a prayer of repentance and faith which has been carefully explained to them have genuinely called on the name of the Lord. No one has ever been saved by reciting a prayer, but many who have been led to recite a prayer have been saved" (from a personal email from Hershael York).

[33] Jeffrey D Johnson, *The Church: Why Bother?* (Birmingham, AL, Solid Ground Books), 20.

a done deal and no matter what happens in people's lives in the decades to follow, even when they are laid six feet under, everyone will talk about how you will see them again in heaven.

Only, for too many, we won't. When spiritually dead people die, all they experience in eternity is a continual dying in the lake of fire with zero hope of escape.[34] The situation is dire. That's why it's so important to learn and believe the *truth* of how salvation works.

The Altar Call and formulaic Sinner's Prayer have done more damage to churches than we can fully realize this side of heaven. *How so?* It creates a system whereby many people see the gospel as a "shot in the arm" they receive to keep them out of hell.[35] And once they get the shot, they don't see a reason to really worry about salvation anymore. "Oh I *know* I'm saved. I've got the date written down in my Bible."

We would be alarmed to see how many people have come forward at the end of a service, have been asked some hurried questions as soft or emotive music is playing, repeated a prayer, but never passed from death to life. They've already said the prayer, so a daily commitment to taking up their cross and following Jesus is not necessary.[36] Instead, they believe, "Hey! I've got my ticket to heaven!

They are the walking dead. We would be stunned at how many people have a date written down in their Bible but not

[34] Revelation 21:8
[35] I first heard a similar analogy to this from a Paul Washer sermon.
[36] Luke 9:23

their name in the Lamb's Book of Life.[37] Even more alarming is how many of these people might be pastors, deacons, Sunday school teachers, or other prominent leaders within the church.[38] Just because people *feel* saved, doesn't mean they *are* saved.[39] This is not a scare tactic, but a plea for us to be serious about the gravity of our predicament. The time for change is right now.

Now that we have diagnosed the problem of false conversions, and the path that led us here, in the following chapters we will examine the biblical truth of how salvation works. It is my sincere prayer that this information will aid us in truly reaching people for Christ instead of adding more people to the list of false converts on a church roll somewhere.

It's time to intentionally, prayerfully, and strategically eliminate the great zombie hordes among us—not by killing them off but by seeing them brought from death to life, one by one. And if they won't join us then at least loving them enough to show them the dreadfulness of their current status before God and the hopelessness of their eternity should they continue to live in rebellion against their most holy and benevolent Creator.

Shouldn't this be a serious burden to us all? It's possible that you're reading this and recognize that there are actually people you've misled in their coming to Christ (I'm guilty too). Or it's

---

[37] See Philippians 4:3, Revelation 20:15

[38] I think we must carefully heed Jesus' warning at the end of the Sermon on the Mount: Matthew 7:21-23. Unconverted leaders in a church impede the growth of true Christians.

[39] Likewise, we can *feel* unsaved and actually be saved. See chapters 5-6.

possible that you're reading this and are a person who had some sort of emotional experience, but you aren't a genuine Christian.

You must remember that the human heart is willing to do almost anything to appease its guilt.[40] It feels guilty and looks for an outlet to alleviate that guilt. With this, combined with the genuine zeal of seeing more people saved, we have created the perfect storm of easy believism.

This isn't meant to frighten us out of evangelizing or to make one *unnecessarily* doubt his or her conversion. It is an admonition to take seriously Scripture's teaching on this matter. Souls are literally at stake. It is time for serious reflection and a sincere willingness to live by genuine biblical principles. Because Scripture is sufficient for our doctrine *and* methodology, let us resolve to let Scripture's authority rank above everything else we encounter regarding this subject.

Let's get to a point where we say, "Enough is enough." Let's be willing to search the Scriptures and take a stand for doing all we can to avoid people falsely professing Christ. Let's be concerned enough for the glory of the Almighty God and the souls of men that we do our best to limit false professions of faith in our day.

Yes, false professions have *always* been a problem. The Apostle Peter dealt with it.[41] The Apostle Paul had to deal with it.[42] Jesus often dealt with it.[43] We will not ever *fully* eliminate

[40] Jeremiah 17:9
[41] Acts 8:18ff
[42] 2 Timothy 4:10
[43] John 2:23-25, John 6:66, John 17:12

false conversions in this life, but we sure can make a better attempt at fixing the current church culture that fosters such large numbers of people who claim to know Christ, but in reality, are walking dead people.

The diagnosis has been given. Now it's time to seek the cure. How does salvation work? Much more could be said, but I've narrowed this down to five main points in the chapters that follow:

- The gospel must be proclaimed,

- God must move,

- the sinner must respond in faith and repentance,

- God justifies the sinner, and

- the sinner grows in the Lord over a lifetime.

Let us be diligent in faithfulness to Christ's teaching on this subject. Let's examine how a person moves from death to life. Let's carefully think through how salvation works. Let's embrace our responsibility in turning the tide.

If we want to see thriving churches in America full of living, fruitful people, then this matters. If we care at all about the glory of God, then this matters. It's not merely a profitable exercise, but a duty.

3

No News Is Bad News

"Go into all the world and preach the gospel."

Jesus[1]

Can you imagine a surprise birthday party without the guest of honor? You've diligently worked behind the scenes to plan the perfect event. The invitations to the guests have been sent out. The balloons are ready. The cake is amazing. The clown, juggling flaming chainsaws, is a little overwhelming, but all in all, everything has been flawlessly executed. Except, the birthday boy doesn't show. Why?

You failed to invite him! No letter. No text message. No phone call. Somehow, in all of your hustle and bustle, you forgot that your friend had no way of knowing to show up at 1010 Memory Lane on Saturday afternoon at 4 o'clock unless someone *communicated* this information to him. He wasn't going to coincidently attend his own surprise party without somebody intentionally telling him when and where he needed to be.

All your work came to naught because of your critical mistake in failing to announce the good news of what you had prepared to the person who most needed to hear it.

[1] Mark 16:15

Announcements like this are crucial. A spiritual announcement is even more crucial.

Step One: We Must Hear the Gospel

When it comes to sinners passing from death to life there is nothing more critical than telling them the good news of Jesus Christ. No news is *bad* news, in this case, for no one will show up to heaven without understanding the gospel—the good news of Christ.

Sinners must be exposed to the gospel to be saved. No one is saved apart from that. This is step one in how salvation works.[2] In the span of eight verses in 1 Thessalonians 2 we have at least four different words used for communicating the gospel. Paul says he and his companions *declared, spoke, shared,* and *proclaimed* the gospel of God to the people of Thessalonica.[3] The result? Many "turned to God from idols to serve the living and true God."[4] God used the gospel message to bring sinners from death to life. He still does.

We must proclaim the gospel; we must send out the invitation to come. Proclaiming the gospel is *telling others* about the good news of Christ. That's all. It might be in a coffee shop, during family devotions, at a hospital bedside, in a Walmart

[2] As we outline these steps throughout the book this should not make us think of salvation as a *process* whereby people are sort of converted and sort of not converted. The point is trying to "zoom in" and carefully think through each element of how a person passes from death to life.

[3] 1 Thessalonians 2:2-9

[4] 1 Thessalonians 1:9

parking lot, or even in a Sunday morning church service. It might be via a tract, text message, or Facebook post.

No news is bad news, indeed. Without the gospel, no one will be saved. Without it, people will go to hell. It's as simple as that.

We may determine when and if we share this good news, but we do not determine the outcome. Sometimes people respond in faith immediately after hearing the word proclaimed. Sometimes it takes longer, and sometimes it happens after one has heard it 999 times before! Sadly, sometimes people hear the word of God and never respond positively. But the point remains: Unless sinners are exposed to the gospel, they will not be saved.

Saying that step one is gospel proclamation does not discount the eternal plan of Almighty God to save sinners for His glory.[5] We could just as easily have said that step one is God's decree in eternity past to save a people for Himself out of the fallen human race. In this book, however, it is our main task to focus on our responsibility to believe the gospel, and to proclaim it to others.

Both are true. God is sovereign. We are responsible.

We would do well to remind ourselves that God is not *obligated* to save *anyone.* Of our own will, we choose to rebel against Him. No one seeks after God, but God has eternally chosen to save sinners through the work of His Son.[6] If not for

[5] See *Baptist Faith and Message* (2000), God's Purpose of Grace.
[6] Romans 3:11

the eternal decrees of God, no one would be saved. Salvation is all of grace and all people who pass from death to life can rightly say that their redemption was determined before the foundation of the world when God chose to save them.[7]

Nothing in me deserves God's saving me, but He chose to show His grace to me anyway. It's God's grace that saves, for sure, but this grace works in and *through* the proclamation of the gospel.[8] "Faith come by *hearing*" the good news of Jesus.[9]

What Is the True Gospel?

If we are saved through hearing the gospel, then it is imperative to define the true gospel. What is it? What do we tell others about it? Do we understand it ourselves?

It is of supreme importance that the gospel we proclaim is derived from Scripture alone. We don't get to say "I think the gospel is..." *Nope.* It doesn't matter what someone *thinks* the gospel is. What matters is Scripture's revelation, for that alone is the gospel truth (pun intended).

The gospel is an announcement. Obtaining salvation is not the result of anything we must *do* but is because of something that has already been done for us.

---

[7] Ephesians 1:3-14, Ephesians 2:8-9. It would not be an unfruitful study to look up how many times the word elect/chosen is used in the New Testament. Here are some examples: Matthew 22:14, Mark 13:27, Romans 8:28-33, 2 Timothy 2:10, Titus 1:1, 1 Peter 1:1-2; 2:9, Revelation 17:14

[8] Ephesians 1:13

[9] Romans 10:17 (emphasis min). No one is saved via dreams, visions in the sky, or some other means. It is only by exposure to the gospel as revealed in the Word of God.

It is *the good news*. Of course, not all good news is the gospel. Drew Carey telling you you've won a "New car!" is good news, but it's not the gospel. So, what exactly is the good news of the gospel? Much ink has already been spilt on this subject, but I think it essential in our endeavor to take a few moments to define the saving message of Jesus Christ.

Before we get to the good news, we need to start with the bad news. In the beginning, God created the heavens and the earth and all was very good, for the first two chapters of the Bible. In Genesis 3, the first man Adam, the representative of all humanity, chose to disobey God.[10] Adam's disobedience carries cosmic significance.

Genesis 3 took place at a real moment in history in a real geographical location but it was far from an isolated event. None of us will ever see Eden again in this life. That ship has sailed because our representative rebelled against a holy God. Because of Adam's guilt, all humanity is born guilty, separated from God.[11]

However, that's not the end of it. We have each personally fallen woefully short of God's glory because we commit our own willful rebellious acts against God.[12] We choose to *sin* because

---

[10] Genesis 3:6

[11] Romans 5:12, 1 Corinthians 15:21-22. Also, we have some tangible examples of representatives that we deal with on almost a daily basis. For example: If a football player hits someone late out of bounds, the whole team gets punished by losing 15 yards. If my child destroys someone else's property, I am responsible for reparation. I never get to talk to the owner of my bank, but only a representative of the bank.

[12] Romans 3:23

we want to follow *our* desires, and not God's commands. John MacArthur defines sin this way:

> Sin is any lack of conformity to God's will in attitude, thought, or action, whether committed actively or passively. The center of all sin is autonomy, which is the replacing of God with self. Always closely associated with sin are its products – pride, selfishness, idolatry, and lack of peace.[13]

Sin permeating our lives is a major problem. How has sin affected man? Only in every conceivable way.

- It has affected our minds.[14]

- It has affected our hearts.[15]

- It has affected our wills.[16]

- It has rendered us unwilling and unable to submit to God.[17]

- It has left us in a state of spiritual deadness.[18]

The Bible teaches that every single part of our lives is tainted by the effects of sin. Not every single person is as sinful as they could possibly be, but every single person is affected by sin from head to toe.

---

[13] John MacArthur and Richard Mayhue, ed. *Biblical Doctrine: A Systematic Summary of Bible Truth* (Wheaton: Crossway, 2017), 454.

[14] Titus 1:15

[15] Jeremiah 17:9

[16] Romans 3:11

[17] Romans 8:7-8

[18] Ephesians 2:1

We are *sinners*. Furthermore, this has obliterated our relationship with God. We have all broken God's Holy Law and deserve His justice.

Psalm 5:5 and Psalm 11:5 both use strong language for God's disposition toward sinners. *Because* God is good, He has a holy and righteous hatred toward sin.[19] It is true that He has no delight in the death of the wicked,[20] but this doesn't mean He will compromise His own holy character in order to have fellowship with sinners. We aren't so cute and loveable that He will tarnish His own glory to rescue us.[21] If God ceased to be Holy, He would cease to be God, and this is impossible. He will one day righteously judge the nations and in so doing will send many to a just eternity in hell.[22] It's what we all deserve. No one can second-guess Almighty God.

This is *very* bad news. Not only are we separated from God by our sin[23] but we are also unwilling and unable to reconcile ourselves to God by any good thing that we can do. We are guilty, vile, and helpless.[24] We are inventors of evil.[25] We are insurgents against God and we don't care. In fact, we refuse to

[19] Psalm 89:14

[20] Ezekiel 33:11

[21] Isaiah 42:8

[22] The greatest problem all mankind faces is that one day, if nothing changes, they will have to forever face the righteous wrath of God. You sometimes see a cartoonish red-suited devil with a pitchfork laughing in hell. But the reality is, he and his angels, along with a multitude of men and women, will burn forever in the lake of fire because of their willful rebellion against a holy God (Revelation 20:10).

[23] Isaiah 59:2

[24] See the hymn "*Man of Sorrows,*" *What a Name*, Philip P. Bliss.

[25] Romans 1:30

acknowledge the full ramifications of our predicament by thinking God will accept us because we do "good deeds" every now and then. Yet, Scripture tells us the very *best* a person can do is considered filthy rags[26] before God, not to mention the worst we do.[27] We are rebels without a clue.

The prerequisite to standing in the presence of the one true, holy, sovereign, triune God of the universe on the Last Day is *righteousness*. The problem? We have no inherent righteousness.

An unrighteous person cannot suddenly become righteous by his own doing. We are not unrighteous merely because of external acts; it's our very nature![28] Men *love* darkness.[29] There is absolutely zero hope of doing enough good to outweigh the bad we've already done.

First of all, we don't really want to do good by God's standards. Secondly, we couldn't do it even if we wanted to because sin has tainted both our heart and mind.[30] Finally, even if you started being perfectly righteous from this point forward, it could never erase the debt we already owe for our past rebellion. What a dilemma.

That's the bad news. What can be done about it? Left to ourselves: *Nothing*. That's why no news is *bad* news.

---

[26] Isaiah 64:6

[27] Dan Phillips, *The World Tilting Gospel* (Grand Rapids: Kregel, 2011), 58-59.

[28] Romans 3:10-18, Jeremiah 17:9. There is nothing intrinsically lovely about us that will prevent God from eternally condemning us.

[29] John 3:19

[30] Romans 8:7-8

The truth we've just walked through is truth whether one accepts it or not.[31] Even if no one ever hears it, it's still true, and remains the hopeless reality for all sinners. *But God...* Two of the greatest words in all of Scripture![32]

Let me show you what I mean. Because of Adam's sin, all humanity deserves an eternity in hell facing God's justice forever. *But God . . .* had a different plan. Hallelujah!

The *good* news is that God did not see fit to leave us in such a condition even though we deserve it. In His infinite wisdom, He devised a plan in eternity past that would uphold His justice while also displaying His grace.[33]

The good news of the gospel is that God has executed His plan to perfection in executing Jesus who is to us both a scapegoat and a perfect sin offering.[34] In Christ there is forgiveness of sins for all those who will repent and believe. He is the only hope of reconciliation between God and man because of His perfect life, vicarious death on the cross, and victorious resurrection.

---

[31] Furthermore, it helps no one to withhold this bad news. It does not matter if someone thinks it is too negative. If we don't understand the bad news, we will never come under conviction of personal sin and come to Christ in saving faith.

[32] Ephesians 2:4

[33] Acts 4:28, Ephesians 1:11

[34] These allude to the theological concepts of expiation and propitiation. Expiation has to do with God taking away our guilt through Jesus and propitiation has to do with God's wrath being satisfied in Jesus's sacrifice.

How Is This Possible?

Adam represented all humanity and failed. Jesus is referred to as *the Second Adam* sent to be a perfect representative.[35] In the third chapter of Genesis, immediately after Adam messed everything up, God promised that He would send someone, born of the seed of the woman, to bruise the Serpent's head.[36] Turns out, that someone would be God Himself, the 2nd Person of the Trinity, the Son, Jesus Christ.[37] The entire Old Testament points to Jesus as God's long-awaited Messiah who would rescue His people from their sins.[38]

God the Father sent God the Son, who stepped into creation conceived by the Holy Spirit, taking on a human body, and beginning humbly as an embryo in the womb of a virgin named Mary. Jesus humbled Himself to be born as a baby, thus was fully man as well as fully God—the God-man.

In His incarnation, he took on a human mind, will, and nature while never giving up His Divine mind, will, or nature. He is now, therefore, properly understood as being 100% God and 100% Man, two distinct natures in only one person.

Only man can make amends for man's rebellion. The problem? All men are wretchedly sinful and miserably insufficient for such a monumental task. *But God,* in His love,

---

[35] 1 Corinthians 15:20-28

[36] Genesis 3:15

[37] Isaiah 9:6 (See Isaiah 44:6 as compared to Revelation 22:13)

[38] Matthew 1:21, Luke 24:27

mercy, justice, and wisdom, provided the solution to the problem.[39]

The Son of God took on human flesh and set aside the splendors of heaven to live among us.[40] As one of my favorite Christmas hymns says:

> *Christ, by highest Heav'n adored; Christ the everlasting Lord;*
> *Late in time, behold Him come, Offspring of a virgin's womb.*
> *Veiled in flesh the Godhead see; Hail th'incarnate Deity,*
> *Pleased with us in flesh to dwell, Jesus our Emmanuel.*[41]

Jesus did not live among us to be a mere *example* but to proclaim to us His fulfillment of all God promised from Genesis 3:15 onward.[42] That fulfillment included His coming to die for our sins and to become our righteousness.[43] He lived a perfect life of obedience to the Law, which no man has or ever could accomplish, and then died a substitutionary, propitiatory death on the cross so that whosoever would believe on Him would be saved.[44]

What that means is that on the cross Jesus was treated as a sinner, though He never sinned, so that we could be treated as righteous, though we have no righteousness of our own. It's really even greater than that! On the cross Jesus didn't merely die *for* us, but He died *as* us in the sense that God literally made

[39] Hebrews 10:5-7
[40] Philippians 2:5-11
[41] Verse 2 of *Hark the Herald Angels Sing* by Charles Wesley (1739).
[42] Matthew 5:17
[43] 1 Peter 2:24, 3:18
[44] 1 John 2:2. He bore the wrath of God for our sins.

Him to be sin, who knew no sin.[45] Jesus made amends for our rebellion. He was our perfect representative.

God punished Jesus instead of me, because Jesus represented me, just like Adam represented me. This is true for any person who places his or her faith in Christ. Jesus was raised for our justification, ascended into heaven, and is now seated at the right hand of the Father, ruling and reigning.[46] On the cross Jesus cried, "It is finished," and we can be assured that not one drop of His blood was shed in vain.[47] He laid down His life for His sheep.[48] Jesus drank, for us, the cup of the wrath of Almighty God down to the last dreg.[49] He didn't just die so that men might *potentially* be saved, but to secure that salvation for all His sheep whom the Father gave Him.[50]

As the song says, He "rose victorious in the strife for those He came to save."[51] His death was truly *sufficient* for the sins of the whole world, but is *effectual* for all who actually repent and believe the gospel, because Christ perfectly secured their salvation as their perfect representative.[52] The wrath of God fell upon Christ instead of us. Our sin went to Him and His righteousness is available to all who will have it by faith.

The gospel announcement is deep, wide, rich, and full but also very simple: "*God saves sinners through the life, death, and*

[45] 2 Corinthians 5:21
[46] Romans 4:25
[47] John 19:30
[48] John 10:7-18
[49] Psalm 75:8
[50] John 10:25-29
[51] *Crown Him with Many Crowns,* Matthew Bridges.
[52] Ephesians 5:25

resurrection of Jesus Christ."[53] God is the holy and righteous Creator. Man lives in fallen rebellion. Jesus lived a perfect life and died the substitutionary death on the cross for sinners, and was raised again in accordance with the Scriptures.

That's the gospel. The gospel is Trinitarian, meaning all three persons of the Trinity are involved. We've looked at the roles of the Father and Son in salvation. In the next chapter, we'll examine the work of the Holy Spirit.

The triune God has worked eternally, sovereignly, and perfectly to accomplish our redemption. All three persons of the Trinity work in harmonious union so that we can rightly and joyfully say, "we are saved from God to God by God through God for God" via gospel proclamation.[54]

No one is saved based on a mere announcement of "Jesus loves you." It's not as simple as following a few basic rules, like, "don't have sex before you're married," or, "don't kill anyone," or, "love your neighbor." It's much more than that. There's truth in those exhortations, obviously, but none of those things will save you; none of them contain the hope of Christ.

If God loves me, but doesn't do anything about my sin, what kind of hope does that leave for me? If I'm told to do better or love better or not do certain things but have no power to carry this out, how is this good news? If I am not told how my past, present, and future sins have been dealt with, how can I ever truly move forward? Christ must be preached. He is the hope

---

[53] Jared Wilson, *Gospel Deeps: Reveling in the Excellencies of Jesus* (Wheaton: Crossway, 2012), 196.

[54] *Ibid.*, 75.

of the nations.[55] He is our perfect Substitute. His death was purposed to bring us *to* God.[56]

Gospel Proclamation

God saves through the proclamation of the gospel, but this doesn't mean that we must fully explain the innumerable riches of the gospel in every evangelistic conversation, for who could ever finish proclaiming such endless treasures? In fact, the gospel is so extensively colossal that it would take mankind longer than eternity to exhaust its magnanimous riches.[57]

Though we never convey *everything* we could possibly say about the gospel and its results, God is gracious to use fallible men and women nonetheless to share His message and to use that very proclamation to bring sinners from death to life. With that being said, let me be crystal clear here: it is the *true gospel* which we just defined that must be proclaimed.[58] This includes the reality of our rebellion against God and the truth of His making atonement for our sin through the life, death, burial, and resurrection of His Son.[59]

Am I saying that we are required to become Bible scholars before we can be saved? Of course not. But we do need to understand the basic tenets of the gospel message:

---

[55] Luke 2:10

[56] 1 Peter 3:18.

[57] I recommend Milton Vincent's *A Gospel Primer for Christians* (Bemidji, MN: Focus Publishing, 2008).

[58] Galatians 1:9

[59] 1 Corinthians 15:1-3, Galatians 1:9

- Though created in God's image, we are sinners from birth and cannot attain to any righteousness of our own; We choose to sin in accordance with our nature.

- If we are to escape condemnation to an eternity in hell, we *must* have a Savior;

- That Savior is the God-man Jesus Christ, our Lord; He lived a perfect life under God's Law, died on the cross as our substitute, and rose again from the grave.

- And only by faith alone in Him alone will we receive His righteousness, and enter into perfect fellowship with all three persons of the Trinity.

This is the gospel message we must clearly articulate to others. Part of communicating the gospel is telling them about the bad news—that we have all sinned and fallen short of the glory of God.[60] People cannot understand their need for Christ until they understand their guilt and righteous condemnation before a Holy God, and no one will savingly believe on Christ if they do not feel a need for Him. J.C. Ryle words this superbly: "Without thorough conviction of sin, men may seem to come to Jesus and follow Him for a season, but they will soon fall away and return to the world."[61]

However, the gospel is about more than just the bad news. Once we establish that, we must move on to the good news. We must clearly share what God has done about our rebellion in

---

[60] Romans 3:23
[61] J.C. Ryle, *Holiness* (Faverdale, UK: EP Books, 1979), 10.

Christ.[62] We broke the Law but Christ kept it, died on the cross for our sins, and rose again.

Finally, this declaration must also include a *call* to the sinner for what he or she must do, namely repent and believe this gospel.[63] Yes, the gospel tells us what Christ has done for us. It's crucial for us to know that.

However, gospel *proclamation* also pleads with the sinner to come to believe in Christ as his or her only suitable and all sufficient Savior.[64] We must herald the truth that God *commands* all men everywhere to repent.[65]

We haven't finished *proclaiming* the gospel until we include what is demanded of the people hearing it—repentance from sin and faith in Christ. God doesn't save sinners on their own terms. They must make peace with Him on His.

A full presentation of the gospel doesn't merely state the bare facts and walk away, but it also invites, pleads, compels, and commands sinners to repent of their rebellion against God and place their faith in Christ.

Avoid Fake News

It's worth noting again that the gospel is the news about how Christ bore our sins to reconcile us to a holy God.[66] In that way, He secured our freedom in Him from every ounce of God's

---

[62] Romans 3:24-25
[63] Mark 1:15
[64] 2 Corinthians 5:11
[65] Acts 17:30
[66] Hebrews 7:27

condemnation. Salvation does not promise every day to be a Friday. It is not a secret weapon to getting our next promotion. It is not a get-rich-quick scheme. It does not promise a cancer-free life. It does not guarantee a life without adversity or trials. It is not the key to unlock untold material blessings. In fact, it promises that "in the world you will have tribulation."[67]

The prosperity gospel we hear so much of today is only "fake news."[68] This false gospel actually leads people *away* from the true gospel. Besides, *all* of these temporal, insignificant promises pale in comparison to what we are offered in the true gospel of Christ.

We don't come to Jesus to get treasure. *He* is the treasure. The gospel is the good news of what God has done in Christ to secure our way into fellowship with Him. Because of Christ's work on our behalf, Christians can be confident that no matter what happens to us here in this life, God is for us and what awaits us in eternity is ruling and reigning with Christ and His people, forever.[69]

Finally, it's poor wording at best, and an absolute false gospel at worst, to exhort people to "live the gospel."[70] That's fake news too. And it's hopeless.

[67] John 16:33

[68] The prosperity gospel is the idea that Jesus's ministry is about you having your best life *now*.

[69] 2 Timothy 2:12

[70] 2 Thessalonians 1:8 is cited by some as a "proof text" for living the gospel. However, there is a great difference between *obeying what the gospel demands* (faith in Christ and repentance from sin) and "living" it. Only Christ *lived* it. We are called to *believe it,* which produces a *changed* life *as a result* of the gospel.

The gospel is not "Go be a Daniel!" Instead, it's that we *deserved* to be ripped to shreds by lions, but Jesus stepped into the pit for us.

The gospel is not "Conquer your giants!" Instead, it's that the Son of David has slain the giant of sin and cut off its head so that we can be free.

The truth of the matter is that I *can't* live the gospel because I am a sinner. I needed Christ to do that for me. Otherwise, I could have no hope of eternal fellowship with the triune holy God.

This is not to be picky about words, but an exhortation for gospel precision in our language. The gospel is the glorious news of Christ's work for us. Don't twist it, even if it sounds good in a sermon. Proclaim the biblical gospel and see God work.

So, how does salvation work? Step one is gospel proclamation, for without it, no one gets saved. It must be communicated to sinners. No news is *bad* news. No one will show up to heaven without an invitation that gets to them in time.[71]

Of course, we know that not everyone who hears, reads, or even intellectually affirms the gospel is saved. The proclamation of the gospel, therefore, is not *all* that is necessary for a person to move from death to life.

[71] Luke 14:23

What happens next? God must move upon the sinner to open his or her heart to receive this good news. We turn to this truth in our next chapter.

4

A Change of Heart

"Thy Spirit has quickened me, has brought me into a new world as a new creature, has given me spiritual perception, has opened to me thy Word as light, guide, solace, joy."

The Valley of Vision[1]

I've carried around many titles over the years – Christian, husband, father, pastor, Razorback fan – but automobile mechanic has never made the list. When it comes to vehicles, I don't know the difference between a flux capacitor and a windshield wiper blade. If there is anything out of kilter on the family minivan, I'm obligated to take it in somewhere if I ever hope for it to be repaired correctly. *I* must initiate a transaction if I want my van to function properly again. I can't sit at home and expect that a certified mechanic is going to magically appear on my doorstep. It's up to *me* to take the initiative to find a solution for my problem.

This is how thousands of religions throughout the world operate. Most people readily admit that there is a problem with humanity, but it can only be fixed if *you* initiate a resolution. Do,

[1] Arthur Bennett, ed. *The Valley of Vision* (Carlisle, PA: Banner of Truth, 2005), 85.

do, do, and do some more – then hope for the best. You must seek Nirvana. You must knock on doors to be part of the 144,000. You must speak positive words over yourself. You must try your best and hope luck tips the scales in your favor.

The message of Christianity is quite different: not *do,* but *done.* In Christianity, the Mechanic comes to me and fixes my car from an impending catastrophic blow up.

God doesn't stop His plan of salvation after the ascension of Jesus. If He had done that, and waited on us to figure it out, no one would ever be saved. Left to ourselves none of us understand the depth of the problem nor the severity of the situation.

In a pointed passage in Romans 3, Paul paints for us a difficult but necessary picture of the state of all mankind apart from Christ. Quoting from various passages in the Old Testament, he writes in Romans 3:10-18:

None is righteous, no, not one;
no one understands; no one seeks for God.
All have turned aside; together they have become worthless;
no one does good, not even one.
Their throat is an open grave;
they use their tongues to deceive.
The venom of asps is under their lips.
Their mouth is full of curses and bitterness.
Their feet are swift to shed blood;
in their paths are ruin and misery,
and the way of peace they have not known.
There is no fear of God before their eyes.

Left to ourselves we do not fear God, seek God, truly understand God, or care about God at all. By nature, all people resist the gospel because all people are sinners. None is righteous. *No, not one.* No one does good, *not even one.* Without Christ, we don't even want to know the problem, much less possess the means or the desire to fix it ourselves.

So, how does anyone get saved then? With man this is impossible![2] *But God...*

There's that wonderful phrase again. God opens our hearts to understand the gospel. He breaks down the fortress of hostility we have erected to show us the wonders of His grace. God brings about a change of heart in us so that we come to Christ in faith and repentance. God doesn't simply advertise, "come here for a great deal on a new transmission." Rather, He comes and applies the gospel to us. God initiates the proper response.

The proclamation of the gospel is meant to go forth to all men, women, and children.[3] There is no racial, socioeconomic, ethnic, or sin barrier that restricts gospel proclamation. It must be proclaimed to all and all must be told to repent and believe it. We must implore, beseech, and plead with every single person to turn from their sin and turn to Christ, trusting Him alone as their only suitable and all sufficient Savior.

But how does a person actually *get saved*? How does it all work? How does a person move from spiritual death to spiritual

[2] Matthew 19:26
[3] Matthew 28:18-20

life? Why don't all who hear the gospel receive it? Are the ones who are getting saved just smarter or more righteous than the ones who reject it? Why did you come to receive Christ, but your neighbor in similar life circumstances did not?

Step Two: God Initiates the Proper Response

The second step in how a person becomes saved is that God initiates the proper response from the sinner. He brings about a change of heart.[4]

While gospel proclamation is absolutely necessary for salvation, it is not *all* that must happen in order to see someone saved. Something more must transpire.

In fact, every single person who has ever lived and heard the gospel *has* responded to it. And all who ever will hear the gospel *will* respond to it—in one way or the other.

The problem is, because of sin, all mankind responds to it *negatively* unless God intervenes. Left to ourselves (remember Romans 3), our response is one of denial, refusal, and rejection. No one seeks after God.

Instead of running to Jesus in faith we rail against Him, mock Him, and get back to our rebellious lives as quickly as we can. We suppress the truth. Like *The Matrix*, we prefer to take the blue pill and suppress the truth so that we can continue living in our alternate reality.

---

[4] Quite literally, He gives us a *new* heart! (Ezekiel 36:26)

If anyone is to be saved, something must happen to wake us up. Something must happen in a person's heart to go from hating God[5] to loving Him. Something must happen to bring us from death to life. Everyone responds to the gospel, but the only way one will respond *satisfactorily* to the gospel is if God first brings about a change of heart.

In John 6:44, Jesus said, "No one can come to me unless the Father who sent me draws him." This seems pretty straightforward, but early in the history of the church a popular teacher by the name of Pelagius (c. 360-418 AD) took offense at the thought that man needed God's gracious act in order to come to Christ. When we look around the evangelical world today, we notice there are many who seem to be of the same mind as this false teacher.

Pelagius believed that man had everything he needed within himself to come to God on his own. Apparently, Jesus didn't get that memo. Pelagius *pretended* to know what was in man, but Jesus actually *knows* what is in man.[6]

Jesus is right. Though all men have permission, no man, because of our sin, has the ability to come to Him without something happening first. Let's digest this a little further.

Though the gate of salvation stands wide open and all may come and freely drink of the fountain of life, the problem is, that left to ourselves we don't want anything to do with God and we certainly do not desire to submit to His terms for salvation. We

[5] Romans 8:7
[6] John 2:25

cannot come because we will not come. Our natural inclination is not to draw near to God but to hide from Him like our first parents.[7]

Most people won't admit it, but if they do not belong to Christ, they actually hate God.[8] They want nothing to do with Him, with His word, or His church. They do not believe His commands are to be followed, and they believe His people are fanatics. Practically speaking, they live their lives as if there were no God at all. Although the light has come into the world, men would rather live in the darkness of sin.[9] Daryl Wingerd writes:

> Simply put, sinners love their sin more than they want to be saved from it. They love wickedness more than the God who condemns them for it. They are enamored by this world, with its priorities and values, more than by the world to come "in which righteousness dwells" (2 Pet. 3:13). By nature, they are attracted to their guilty pleasures more strongly than they are drawn to Christ, who came to free men from slavery. Sin is what they crave. God, Christ, the gospel of grace, repentance, and righteousness, are what they are repulsed by. Unbelief is willful and worthy of condemnation, not pitiable, justifiable, or excusable.[10]

[7] Genesis 3:8

[8] Romans 1:30. They won't use the word "hate," but it's the same as a man saying he doesn't "hate" his wife all while trying to poison her coffee every morning and sleeping around on her with other women every night. One might say he doesn't "hate" his wife, but if he lived that way everyone would know that in actuality, he does.

[9] John 3:19-20

[10] Daryl Wingerd, http://bulletininserts.org, "You Cannot Because You Will Not, But If You Will, You Can"

Dark is the stain that we cannot hide, but praise God for *His pursuit of us*. Just like He pursued Adam and Eve in the Garden, just like He pursed Abram in Ur, David in Bethlehem, and Saul on the road to Damascus, so too is God still in the act of pursuing rebellious sinners to this day. Aslan is on the move. God is drawing sinners to Himself. Marvelous grace indeed.

Some people confuse this drawing of God by saying God is drawing *every single* sinner to Christ *every single time* the gospel is proclaimed. After all, Jesus says, "And I, if I be lifted up from the earth, will draw all men unto me."[11] So how should we understand this?

This is where we must remember a passage of Scripture can't mean whatever we want it to mean. It must mean what God *intended* it to mean in its context (and that's what we *should want* it to mean).[12]

In John 12:20, we see that Greeks joined the scene to worship. Twelve verses later Jesus clarifies that His death on the cross was in fact a global endeavor. God is saving people all over the world. From Arkansas to Argentina. From Pittsburgh to Pudong. He was referring to effectually drawing Greeks and Jews alike, not every single person who has ever lived.

As D. A. Carson notes, "The context shows rather clearly...that [John] 12:32 refers to 'all men without distinction'

---

[11] John 12:32

[12] As R.C. Sproul said: "It is your duty to believe and to teach what the Bible teaches, not what you want it to teach." https://twitter.com/RCSproul/status/934600309883719680

(i.e. not just Jews) rather than to 'all men without exception'."[13] In other words, the blood of Christ "ransomed people for God from every tribe and language and people and nation."[14] God calls people out of sin from all over the world through the heralding of the gospel.[15] Because of unbelief, many people who hear the gospel will not embrace it. But the good news of God's work is that He's doing something about that in the lives of many others.

The reason many are *not* saved is not the fault of God, nor is it because of some insufficiency in the death of Christ. Rather, it is because all men, women, boys, and girls are sinners. William Gurnall (1616 – 1679) rightly summarizes this reality: "If you enter eternity with a hard, impenitent heart, you have no one to blame but yourself."[16]

Left to ourselves, we don't want Christ, and God has justly given many over to exactly what they most want.[17] God is not obligated to draw lost persons to Himself. He has no obligation to show mercy and grace to sinners, for if He did, it would no longer be mercy or grace. Mercy and grace are, by definition,

[13] D.A. Carson, *The Gospel According to John* (Leicester, UK: Intervarsity Press, 1991), 293. Later, Carson notes: "Here, [John 12:32] 'all men' reminds the reader of what triggered these statements, *viz.* the arrival of the Greeks, and means 'all people without distinction, Jews and Gentiles alike', not all individuals without exception, since the surrounding context has just established judgment as a major theme (v. 31)," 444. (i.e., context matters)

[14] Revelation 5:9

[15] Acts 13:48

[16] William Gurnall, *The Christian in Complete Armour*, Vol. 1 (Carlisle, PA: Banner of Truth, 1986), 224.

[17] Psalm 81:12, Romans 1:24

unearned and undeserved.[18] No one seeks after God and He is perfectly just in leaving people to their *own choice* of rejecting Him.

Yes, the door of salvation stands wide open, but many will never find it because of their own unwillingness and cold, resistant hearts. As John Calvin wrote "No man is excluded from calling upon God, the gate of salvation is set open unto all men: neither is there any other thing which keepeth us back from entering in, save only our own unbelief."[19]

God *could* turn on the lights in their heart, but He has chosen to leave them to their *own choice* of sin and death. This penalty for rebellion is right and just. But because of God's amazing grace, it is not that way for all.

We see this concept clearly taught in the Bible, but we also see it unfold during evangelistic encounters. When you share the gospel, have you noticed how many are *completely unmoved and unresponsive* to it? You may proclaim the glorious news of the death of Christ for sinners to a group of people you know are lost and some respond by saying, "Did you see that ballgame last night?"

Or when you passionately pour out the gospel to your 7-year-old and she responds with, "Can we have pizza for supper?" The opposite example holds true too: I prayed for my dad, and shared the gospel with him, for about fifteen years before he

---

[18] R.C. Sproul, *The Holiness of God* (Grand Rapids: Tyndale, 1998), 155.

[19] Calvin's Commentaries, Vol. 36: Acts, Part I, tr. by John King, [1847-50], at sacred-texts.com (Acts 2:14-21).

became a Christian. What finally happened? God changed his heart.

The point here is, unless God brings about a change of heart in the sinner, no one responds positively to the gospel. Think through this for just a moment. Suppose someone says to you, "I've had a change of heart. I'm now a Christian." *How* did this change of heart happen?

Did this person finally get smart enough? Did they finally make up their mind that they didn't like sin? Did they evaluate all the evidence in front of them and conclude that following Jesus was the wisest course of action? If the answer is "yes" to any of those questions, then they haven't been saved by *grace* but by something they've done.[20] This would reduce evangelism merely to convincing people to activate their inner "faith muscle" and grab the rope as the life preserver is thrown to them.

Actually, some evangelistic tactics are geared toward just that, aren't they? But the biblical reality is that by nature, we all reject the light of the gospel.[21] We are perfectly content following the imaginary god we've created in our own fallen minds—patterned after ourselves in most cases. The god we create is certainly not the God of the Bible. No way do we want to exchange our fantasy world for submission to the King of kings.

So this isn't God keeping people from Him. This is God giving people over to choose what they really want: sin.[22] No one

---

[20] Romans 11:6
[21] John 3:19
[22] Romans 1:28

will truly call Jesus, "Lord," (and live as though He really is) except by the Spirit of God.[23]

If we hope to truly comprehend how salvation works, we must understand the priority of God's acting upon the sinner. He must draw them to Himself. Certainly, God's drawing includes a conviction of sin and a pressing upon the heart and mind of the need for Christ. But it entails even more: this effectual drawing is the regenerating work of the Holy Spirit. It is a literal change of heart.

You remember John 6:44? Jesus says those He draws, He *will raise up* on the last day. This is a potent and decisive drawing. Consider what the Baptist Faith and Message 2000 says:

> Regeneration, or the new birth, is a work of God's grace whereby believers become new creatures in Christ Jesus. It is a change of heart *wrought by the Holy Spirit* through conviction of sin, to which the sinner responds in repentance toward God and faith in the Lord Jesus Christ. Repentance and faith are inseparable experiences of grace. (Emphasis mine)

There is much to unpack in that passage, but notice the line, "It is a change of heart *wrought by the Holy Spirit* through conviction of sin, to which the sinner *responds* in repentance toward God and faith in ...Christ." God initiates and the sinner responds. That's clear.

[23] 1 Corinthians 12:3

The sinner doesn't draw God. God draws the sinner. God is not responding to the sinner at this point, rather the sinner responds to God.

Regeneration is not a cooperative effort.[24] It's not "you make the first step and God will do the rest." That would be hopeless, for none of us would ever budge an inch. "So then it depends not on human will or exertion, but on God, who has mercy."[25]

So, the gospel is proclaimed, the Holy Spirit creates a new heart in the sinner and God enables him/her to respond in repentance and faith. If He doesn't do this work in the sinner's heart, that person remains in his state of sin and rejects Christ.[26] If God *does* do a work in the heart, it is an act of His sheer mercy and grace alone, not based on anything good in that person.[27] We are not saved because we are worthy. We are saved because He is merciful.

Furthermore, this work isn't God dragging unwilling sinners to Him. Rather, He opens their eyes to see the reality of their sin and that their only hope of salvation is Christ so that in response they freely run to Him in repentance and faith (see next chapter). The sinner's heart of stone melts under the

---

[24] Noted theologian, J.I. Packer, says it this way: "Regeneration is the spiritual change wrought in the heart of man by the Holy Spirit in which his/her inherently sinful nature is changed so that he/she can respond to God in Faith, and live in accordance with His Will. It extends to the whole nature of man, altering his governing disposition, illuminating his mind, freeing his will, and renewing his nature." https://www.monergism.com/thethreshold/articles/onsite/packer_regen.html

[25] Romans 9:16

[26] John 3:18

[27] 1 Peter 1:3, Titus 3:5

gracious power of God and, for the first time, he or she sees Christ as an inestimable treasure and the pearl of great price.[28]

The Bible is straightforward about God's initiating work in salvation as He draws us to Himself and causes us to be born again by the power of the Holy Spirit.[29] This isn't something hidden in some obscure passage of Scripture. It's not relegated to the footnotes. It's everywhere! Here are three different texts by three different New Testament authors:

- He who *began a good work in you* will bring it to completion at the day of Jesus Christ.[30]

- *Of his own will he brought us forth by the word of truth...*[31]

- Everyone who believes that Jesus is the Christ *has been born of God.*[32]

The grand narrative of the Bible itself is sinful man rejecting Holy God and God pursuing man for His own eternal glory. God's initiating work is described throughout Scripture.

God initiates the work of salvation. These verses do not say, okay, God did *His* part, now you've got to do yours. Wrong. He *causes* us to be born again according to His *mercy* – not our "taking the first step."[33] The necessity of God's initiating work

---

[28] Matthew 13:44-46

[29] See another example in Acts 10:44

[30] Philippians 1:6, emphasis mine.

[31] James 1:18a, emphasis mine.

[32] 1 John 5:1, emphasis mine. Belief is in response to being born again (see also 1 John 3:9a).

[33] 1 Peter 1:3

isn't really all that difficult to discover or understand but, to the prideful heart, it's hard to accept.

At my core, I do not want to believe that I am not in control. I do not like to think of my *free will* as an enslavement to my own sinful cravings and desires.[34] I want to be completely autonomous. I want to be king. I want to be god. It's my nature to rebel.

But that's where the gospel of grace comes in and humbles us. It shows us that none would ever choose Jesus, apart from God's grace. We've all gone our own way and we are rebellious, hopeless, and helpless.[35] It doesn't matter how many prayers one prays, how sincere they seem, or how committed one initially appears to be to the things of Christ. If God isn't working, conversion will always be false because, without the work of God in their hearts, people simply do what they think it will take to get God off their back and get back to the life they want to live, without guilt or shame.

Many people appear to be true believers for a time, but eventually the cares of this world or the fear of rejection and persecution will show them to be false converts.[36] Or, worse, they will continue to deceive everyone around them until Jesus exposes them on the Day of Judgment.[37]

Again, God's heart-changing grace isn't easy for men to accept. Jesus taught on this matter in John 6 and, as a result,

---

[34] John 8:34
[35] Isaiah 53:6
[36] Matthew 13:18-23
[37] Matthew 7:21-23, Matthew 25:41-46

many of His disciples left Him.[38] Is mankind really so sinful that God must move first in people's lives before they will ever respond positively to the gospel? Unequivocally, yes.

No guilt trip, scare tactic, tiger on stage, compelling video, or fifteen stanzas of *Just as I Am* will bring a sinner to Christ. The gospel must be proclaimed and God must move in such a way as to evoke the required response from the sinner.[39]

So, the issue is not whether this is true, but whether we by faith trust Scripture over tradition or experience? What the Bible says, God says, and when we are trusting Scripture to instruct us in this matter we are saying that God does in fact know what He is talking about. "It is the Bible, not experience, that is the benchmark of truth."[40]

Because of sin, no lost person feels they really need Jesus, and all are unconcerned in living a life of rejecting our most benevolent God. This is why Scripture says, "every one of you *follows* his stubborn, evil will."[41] The will is free to act but is enslaved to sin. A lost person's choice will always be sin over righteousness just like a buzzard's choice will always be rancid meat over salad.

But praise God that He doesn't leave all mankind in such a state! God is the initiator. He is willing and able to break through the hardest of hearts and draw them to Christ. He takes our

---

[38] John 6:63-66

[39] John 1:13, John 6:63

[40] Adrian Rogers, *What Every Christian Ought to Know* (Nashville: B&H, 2012), 361.

[41] Jeremiah 16:12, emphasis mine.

enslaved wills and frees them so that we joyfully run to Him. *No one* is beyond His reach. The fact that God is still in the saving business encourages us to preach the gospel to all people, imploring them to repent and believe, because we know that as we do that, some will come to Christ! Why? Because we're so eloquent? No. They will come because God changes their hearts and draws them to faith in Him.

Understanding this glorious truth emboldens our evangelism like never before. As we pass out tracts, preach to the masses, have a conversation on the airplane, talk with a coworker, or share the gospel with a family member we know that God has the power to bring that person from death to life. We pray confidently, and share boldly because we know that God changes hearts. The result does not depend on us, but on God.

May we be compassionate voices of urgency calling people out of death and into life. This frees us from feeling the need to create a dog and pony show so that people might find Christianity interesting enough to accept it. Instead, we can share the good news of the gospel knowing that Jesus "*will* save His people from their sins."[42] God will turn on the lights in the hearts of people, and He doesn't need you or me to make the gospel more attractive in order to do so.

How does salvation work? The gospel is proclaimed, and through this gospel proclamation God opens hearts, and graciously, sovereignly, and effectually draws sinners to Himself in faith.

---

[42] Matthew 1:21, emphasis mine.

However, that's not all that needs to happen for a person to be saved. God doesn't unduly coerce the sinner into this next step. There must be a conscious, will-induced coming to Christ in faith. If we rightly emphasize the necessity of God's drawing, but do so at the expense of the twin truth that a person freely chooses Christ in response to said drawing, we have unhelpfully distorted the truth of how salvation works. In our next chapter, we'll discuss the required response of repentance and faith.

5

Bare Necessities

*"Let every one that is out of Christ,
now awake and fly from the wrath to come."*
Jonathan Edwards[1]

When my wife and I moved to Louisville, KY for seminary, we learned, through financial necessity, to function with fewer amenities around the house than we first imagined possible. You might say we were living off the bare necessities. Those days were a special time for us as we learned to depend on the Lord and one another.

Think of all the material possessions that we really *could* live without. We wouldn't *want* to do it, but we could survive with much less. Refrigerators, microwaves, toasters, televisions, vacuums, iPhones, and the internet, are just a few examples of commodities that make life much less labor intensive, but aren't required for survival. Then there's the As Seen on TV products, like the *Snuggie* or *Flex Seal,* that you never knew you needed until you saw the commercial. Americans are constantly working harder to make life easier.

[1] Jonathan Edwards, *Sinners in the Hands of an Angry God and Other Puritan Sermons* (Mineola, NY: Dover Publications, 2005), 184.

I love this creativity. It's part of the *Imago Dei.*[2]

Unfortunately, we've gotten *too* creative when it comes to how a person responds to the gospel message. We've become experts on making it "easier" for people to become Christians. We've mastered the sales pitch. Say these words, check this box, sign this card, affirm these facts, and you're in. We've taken the information in the Bible and tried to boil it down to the lowest possible passing grade, the bottom rung on the ladder. What is the least amount of commitment we can require of someone and still be able to count them as converted?

We are like Baloo telling Mowgli to look for the bare necessities, but no matter how long one looks, the simple bare necessities are *always* repentance and faith. No matter how creative we may try to be, the standard does not lower for any person.[3]

The required response to the proclamation of the gospel is complete and total surrender with no negotiation. The only way to be saved is to come to God on His terms. How does salvation work? The gospel is preached, the Spirit quickens,[4] and the sinner properly responds in repentance and faith. The sinner's proper response is the subject of this chapter.

Third Step: The Sinner's Proper Response

Zooming in on how salvation works may lead you to believe that *becoming* a Christian is a series of moments in time, but this

[2] Image of God.
[3] Acts 17:30
[4] John 6:63, KJV

isn't accurate. The events leading to one's salvation may be many, but actually becoming a Christian is an instantaneous event.[5] The takeaway here is that we don't look at the relationship between God's movement upon the sinner (last chapter) and the sinner's response (this chapter) as a series of moments in time.

In actuality, these events occur concurrently. Of course, we must adamantly maintain that God's work always comes *first* in terms of causality. "Regeneration is the *cause*, not the consequence, of saving faith."[6] Lazarus did not come to life *because* he walked out of the tomb. He walked out of the tomb *because* he was brought to life. The Savior initiated this response by His sovereign call.[7] God must initiate the response, or no one would ever come to Christ because of our sinfulness.[8]

---

[5] I don't mean to suggest that we always can pinpoint the day or the hour when we truly came to faith and repentance in Christ. 1.) That's nowhere mentioned in Scripture 2.) We see the great testimony of saints in the church who couldn't pinpoint that moment in time. Yes, it is a moment in time, and yes, some *do* know the day and hour, but to make this a requirement to a true believer is not biblical.

[6] *Biblical Doctrine*, 585 (emphasis mine).

[7] John 11:43-44

[8] MacArthur writes: "In his state of spiritual death (Eph. 2:1-3), man is incapable of even understanding the things of the Spirit, let alone receive them (1 Cor. 2:14). The sinner's mind is so hostile to God that he is literally unable to submit to God's law (Rom. 8:7), and thus he cannot please God in any sense (Rom. 8:8), including the exercise of faith (Heb. 11:6). Man is blind to the value of God' glory revealed in Christ and is hopelessly enamored with sin, despite its worthlessness. To suggest that a sinner in such a state could, apart from the regenerating grace of the Holy Spirit, summon from within his own deadness the saving faith that God declares to be his sovereign gift (Eph. 2:8) is to wholly underestimate the miserable nature of man's depravity" (*Biblical Doctrine*, 586).

When the Holy Spirit moves in a saving way (not merely exposing sin, but actually saying "let there be light" to our hearts[9]) the sinner is brought to life whereby God effects[10] the desired response, i.e. the sinner comes to Christ in saving faith.[11] *He makes us alive.*[12] Apart from this we are dead in our trespasses and sins.[13] Dead men do not talk, walk, or seek God. Clearly we are not physically dead, but we are *spiritually* dead. We are dead in such a way that our hearts are referred to as "stones."[14]

Go ask a rock what it wants for supper. Go preach a sermon at a graveyard. You'll get the same response. The Spirit of God must move upon the sinner. Ask Lazarus his favorite color before Jesus told him to come forth and see what he says: *nothing,* for he "stinketh."[15]

We explored human sinfulness in the last chapter but I think the spiritual deadness of non-Christians is one of the hardest truths for us to grasp. It's hard to grasp because in our experience, we see people all the time seemingly making "spiritual decisions." But the reality is that decisions for Christ aren't merely something we *cannot* do; they are something our own wills *will not* do.[16]

---

[9] 2 Corinthians 4:6

[10] Not *affects*, but effects, as in *achieves.*

[11] Romans 8:30

[12] Ephesians 2:4

[13] Ephesians 2:1

[14] Ezekiel 36:26

[15] John 11:39, KJV

[16] We can't because we won't. And we won't because we don't want to.

It's like trying to get 3-year olds to like broccoli. You can pray for them. You can try to mix it with something else. But unless something changes in their taste buds, they aren't going to enjoy most vegetables. It's who they are.

Who we are apart from Christ is spiritually dead, as in d-e-a-d: inanimate, unmoving, unwilling, a corpse at the bottom of the ocean floor. John Piper correctly writes: "Authentic faith is never a mere human decision that can be made by willpower without a transformed heart."[17]

Therefore, we don't come to Christ with a free will so much as a *freed* will. No one has a "faith muscle" inside of them that simply needs to be exercised in order to come to Christ.

Because of the nature of sin and the reality of our sinful state, God must move first. And when the Holy Spirit moves in this saving way, the sinner *is* made alive, to which he or she *does* cry out to God in saving faith. So, it is not faith that opens our hearts; rather *God* opens our hearts so that we exercise His gift of faith.

Let's examine the Baptist Faith and Message once more:

Regeneration, or the new birth, is a work of God's grace whereby believers become new creatures in Christ Jesus. It is a change of heart wrought by the Holy Spirit *through conviction of sin, to which the sinner responds in repentance toward God and faith in the Lord Jesus Christ.*

We see here the biblical truth that although regeneration is solely God's work, sinners are not passive in their *conversion.*

---

[17] John Piper, *Reading the Bible Supernaturally: Seeing and Savoring the Glory of God in Scripture.* (Wheaton, IL, Crossway, 2017), 124.

They aren't walking down the sidewalk one day getting struck by a bolt of grace lightning only to find out when they die twenty years later that they were saved and never even aware of what happened.

As adamant as we are about God's regenerating work in the hearts of men and women, we must be equally adamant that if a person does not *choose* to repent and believe the gospel, they will not be saved. No one gets saved apart from a personal decision to follow Jesus.

I like to explain it this way: We cannot place ourselves into the spiritual realm and see all that God is doing. In a sense it's none of our business what God is up to. Instead, we must regard what we're commanded to do—to repent and believe the gospel.[18] That's our realm.

God acts. The sinner responds to God's acting. Both are necessary for a person to be saved.

The scope of salvation is not merely regeneration, where God does the work alone. It also entails conversion—the part where we choose to repent and believe the gospel in response to God's effectual work in our hearts.

What Is Biblical Repentance?

When Paul and Silas told the Philippian jailer to "believe on the Lord Jesus and you will be saved" they meant it. No gimmickry or bait and switch was present in their methods. But in no way

[18] Mark 1:15

does this mean that the response the gospel demands is easy or that repentance is optional.[19]

Biblical repentance is necessary for any person to become a Christian. Yes, the weakest faith anchors us to a strong Christ, but even the weakest faith will produce true repentance from sin because repentance is a gift of God.[20] This gift is not a forcing of our wills to repent. Rather it is an opening of our hearts and minds to see that God's way is right and ours is wrong. That's when we, of our own *freed will*, truly and actually repent. God does not and will not repent for us. Anyone who has ever become a Christian has chosen, by grace, to repent of sin.

We still hear the word *repent* used quite often in many faithful evangelical churches. However, sometimes I'm like Inigo Montoya on *The Princess Bride*: "You keep using that word. I do not think it means what you think it means."

So, what is biblical repentance?[21] Repentance is not a mere sorrow for sin or some kind of an acknowledgment of sin. Often

[19] Notice for example, that they told the jailer he must believe on the *Lord* Jesus, implying that this man must submit to Christ recognizing Him as the rightful King of his life.

[20] 2 Timothy 2:25, Acts 11:18. Some people point to the thief on the cross as an example of someone coming to Christ in faith completely separate from repentance. Yet, even in that scenario, the man acknowledged Christ as *King*. He said, "'Jesus, remember me when you come into your *kingdom*." (Luke 23:42, emphasis mine).

[21] Question 92 of the Baptist Catechism asks, "What is repentance unto life?" The answer: "Repentance unto life is a saving grace, whereby a sinner, out of a true sense of his sin, and apprehension of the mercy of God in Christ, doth, with grief and hatred of his sin, turn from it unto God, with full purpose of and endeavor after new obedience." *The Baptist Confession of Faith & The Baptist Catechism.* (Solid Ground Christian Books and Reformed Baptist Publications, 2010), 115.

times the Sinner's Prayer begins with "Dear God, I know that I'm a sinner," to which I think the Lord might reply something like, "Yes, I know. That's why I sent my Son."

Any 5-year old can acknowledge that not picking up his toys when his mom and dad tell him to is wrong. Paul speaks of a worldly sorrow for sin that only produces *death.*[22] We, too, readily assume that a person who cries during an evangelistic encounter must be repentant. It's *possible* they are repentant. Or they may merely feel guilty.

Remorse does not equal repentance. The man on death row feels remorse, perhaps. The child who steals a cookie is sorry when she gets caught, and may even shed a tear. It's not enough just to *know* you're a sinner and feel bad for sinning. We all feel bad for breaking God's Holy Law at various times because we are made in the image of God.

As wicked as our 21st Century culture is, there remain vestiges of understanding in the human heart of right and wrong. This is because the human heart, though fallen, retains enough of the *Imago Dei* to recognize sin at times. It's not enough to admit you are a sinner. Trust me, God already knows that, and He's not pleased—and will not give sinners a pass.[23]

Biblical repentance is changing direction. It involves *turning away* from our sin. It's not a temporary diet of good behavior, but a life transformation. It is a turning from sin and total surrender of oneself to the Lordship of Christ. Repentance

[22] 2 Corinthians 7:10
[23] Psalm 7:11

means the nature of sin is seen for what it is: rebellion against God.

Repentance is then hating sin because it is an attack on the glory of God. It is a change in mindset. It is seeing a new King in one's life: Jesus, the Son of God.

Repentance is not "making" Jesus the Lord of your life. He already is—whether you recognize that or not![24] Rather, it is joyfully acknowledging the Lordship of Christ and bowing the knee, moving from a life of seeking one's autonomy, to one of glad submission to the King of kings and Lord of lords. It's choosing to do what Jesus tells us to do.

Samuel Davies (1723 - 1761) preached:

> To repent, in the language of the Bible, is to depart from our evil ways, to cease to do evil and to learn to do well, to cleanse our hands and purify our hearts; which expressions signify not only sorrow for sin but especially reformation from it. In vain, therefore, do you pretend to repent if you still go on in the sins of which you repent.[25]

Similarly, the 17th Century Puritan, Thomas Watson, lays out six ingredients for true biblical repentance:[26]

---

[24] 2 Corinthians 4:5

[25] Richard Owen Roberts, ed. *Salvation in Full Color: Twenty Sermons by Great Awakening Preachers* (Wheaton, IL: International Awakening Press, 1994), 208.

[26] Thomas Watson, *The Doctrine of Repentance* (Edinburgh: Banner of Truth, 1987). These are Watson's title chapters. The explanations are my own.

1. Sight of Sin – which is an opening of our eyes to seeing sin as sin: dark and vile, and, as R.C. Sproul has famously said, *cosmic treason.*

2. Godly Sorrow for Sin – which is not just a guilty conscience but the true beatitude of gospel mourning.[27] It sees that the death of Christ wasn't merely about "sins" but *my sins.*

3. Confession of Sin – Yes, the admission of guilt for your sins is an important *part* of repentance. It's just not the *only* aspect of repentance that we need to understand.

4. Shame for Sin – Shame, if understood properly, is a good thing.[28] It helps us understand our sin rightly. If we see the holy character of God and understand who we are apart from Him, shame *should* be our response.

5. Hatred of Sin – Repentance is not just giving up sin so we can go to heaven. It is hating sin because it is an offence against God and a detriment to the human race (Proverbs 8:13).

6. Turning from Sin – As mentioned above, repentance entails more than simply acknowledging or confessing sin. It is a true turning in a person's heart away from sin and self. It is choosing to do right instead of wrong. It is actually turning away from *all* known sins. This is a lifelong endeavor.

These ingredients are the bare necessities of repentance. If any of these components are left out, you no longer have biblical repentance. No, *perfect* repentance isn't required, for in our

---

[27] Matthew 5:3-5
[28] 2 Thessalonians 3:13-15

current state we will never perfectly repent. But, *true* repentance *is* required and any imitations of this gospel duty must be rejected. As hard as men have tried, we will never be able to create a system whereby people become Christians apart from true, heart-wrought, and *biblical* repentance.

Because of the character of biblical repentance, we will not see its depth during the end of a worship service or evangelistic conversation. It doesn't work like that. All we can see is a confession of repentance. We won't be able to attest its sincerity until we see how this new life is lived.

Clyde Cranford helps us here: "The evidence that repentance is real is not a display of emotion at conversion, but works which are appropriate to repentance: restitution for wrongs, all forms of Christian service and ministry, and personal spiritual disciplines."[29]

We will address this more closely when we discuss the vital aspect of sanctification. Suffice it to say, true repentance entails more than saying you're sorry or asking for forgiveness.

A person's repentance, or lack thereof, directly correlates to his or her view of God.[30] If we continue to preach a weak and needy god who loves us more than his own glory, then we can expect a deficient understanding of repentance to continue to permeate evangelicalism.

God doesn't need us. We need Him.

---

[29] Clyde Cranford, *Because We Love Him: Embracing a Life of Holiness* (Sisters, OR: Multnomah Publishers, 2002), 87.
[30] Isaiah 6:5

Even the word *need* seems woefully inadequate to describe our situation. He sustains every heartbeat, breath, and molecule in the universe.[31] He is good to all and His common grace restrains men from being as evil as they possibly could be.[32] His patience prevents this evil world from collapsing upon itself. We are desperately dependent on Him for everything.

All of this kindness is meant to lead us to *repentance*.[33] He is so good to His creation, and yet we spit in His Holy face with our sins of commission and omission. We do what God says not to do and we do not do what God says to do. We break His Law and laugh about it, or act as though we will never have to give an account for our actions.

Furthermore, we "tolerate a view of God which is vastly beneath the revelation which God makes of Himself in Holy Scriptures."[34] We are in constant danger of trying to make God out to be like one of us, just a little bit bigger.[35] The Lord of hosts is not like us. He is *Holy, Holy, Holy.*[36] He is eternally triune, Father, Son, and Holy Spirit, One God in three distinct but coequal persons.[37]

When you arrive at the limit of human comprehension, the knowledge of God has not been the least bit exhausted.

---

[31] Colossians 1:17

[32] Psalm 145:9, Matthew 5:45, Genesis 20:6

[33] Romans 2:4

[34] *Salvation in Full Color*, xi.

[35] Psalm 50:21

[36] Isaiah 6:3, Revelation 4:8

[37] While there is not a verse that says "God is trinity" this truth permeates the Bible. We see the entire Trinity present in places like Matthew 3:16-17, Matthew 28:19, and Ephesians 1:3-14. One in essence, three in person.

Righteousness and justice are the foundation of His throne.[38] He is the great and awesome God.[39] At His right hand are pleasures forevermore.[40] He is infinite in wisdom and His knowledge is unsearchable.[41] He is always right, always good, always perfect, and always God most high.[42]

He is sovereign in, through, and over all things and His plans and purposes cannot be thwarted by puny man.[43] A weak, needy, and unholy god demands nothing of our repentance. But the God of the Bible will have no dealings with a person or people who refuse to turn from sin.[44]

How serious is God about sin? *Look at the cross.* His wrath, which was against our disobedience, was poured out on His sinless Son, Jesus Christ.

Thus, we impugn the character of God when we depict Him as being flippant or unconcerned about our sinning. This is why when we proclaim the gospel we dare not truncate it or attempt to make it more palatable to a lost person's ears by diminishing the truth about who God is in all of His glory.

God doesn't beg people to repent so they can be the star player on His team. He *demands* repentance. He owes mankind nothing. What a fearful and insolent game we play by making repentance an optional feature to becoming a Christian,

[38] Psalm 89:14
[39] Nehemiah 1:5
[40] Psalm 16:11
[41] Romans 11:33
[42] Psalm 145:3
[43] Job 42:2, Isaiah 14:27, Jeremiah 32:17, Acts 4:24-28
[44] Joel 2:12, Revelation 16:11

refusing to properly define it in hopes of sneaking people into the kingdom, or by flat out dismissing it altogether.

What Is Saving Faith?

It's important to clear up something right away. It's not faith that saves, but God who saves. There are four important prepositions to remember in all of this—by, through, in, and for. We are saved *by* God alone, *through* faith alone, *in* Christ alone, *for* the glory of God alone.[45]

Faith is the instrument God uses to unite us to all the blessings Christ secured for us in His life, death, burial, and resurrection. Actually, it's even better than that. The way we receive all the blessings of Christ's work is that God unites us to Christ *Himself* through the instrument of saving faith.[46] So, what exactly *is* saving faith?

Saving faith is the other side of repentance. Actually, it's more precise to say that repentance is the other side of saving faith. Coming to Christ in faith will always involve repentance of sin.

As clear as we must be about the necessity of repentance, we don't repent to get to Christ. We come to Christ in saving faith and in so doing we repent. We don't do what's good and right so that Jesus will accept us. Rather, a faith that trusts the gospel longs to do what is good and right. The sinner doesn't merely turn *away* from sin but he turns *to* Christ alone as his only

[45] See, for example, the way Paul explains this in Ephesians 2:8-9 and Philippians 3:9.
[46] Romans 6:5-8

suitable and all sufficient Savior. It is our turning to Christ that leads us to turn away from sin.

Cranford writes, "Christian faith is more than an intellectual assent to certain propositions. It is looking to God. That is why it is so closely linked with repentance. Simply stated, repentance and faith are *turning* and *looking*."[47]

Historically, faith has been understood to have three key aspects. There are facts about Jesus and His work to be understood, a conviction that the gospel is true, and a personal trust in Christ.[48]

All three of these components are necessary for faith to be saving. Does not the devil intellectually know the facts of the gospel? Yes, he does. But he doesn't turn and he doesn't look to God.

Certainly, complete and full agreement with the truth claims of the gospel is a crucial aspect of saving faith, but it does not stop there. It's not just looking at the bridge and affirming that it could get you to the other side. It is actually crossing the bridge.

The bridge is Christ, for Christ alone is the only proper object of saving faith.[49] We can't have faith in faith or merely believe for the sake of believing. We must have faith *in* Christ.

---

[47] *Because We Love Him*, 89.

[48] This sentence is a rewording of notes from a sermon preached by Scott Lee, pastor of Rockport Baptist Church in Arnold, MO. It is a summary of the classic magisterial reformers' explanation of faith using the Latin words *notitia*, *assensus*, and *fiducia*. See https://www.ligonier.org/learn/devotionals/three-aspects-of-faith/ for more.

[49] John 6:40

We must believe *on* Christ. We must lean on Him.[50] We must not merely know the facts about Christ but put the full weight of our hope for eternal life upon Him.

Furthermore, this is not a corporate faith, but a personal one. *You* must believe on Christ.[51] "It will not save me to know that Christ is a Saviour; but it will save me to *trust* him to be *my* Saviour."[52]

The nature of saving faith is simple enough for even a small child to understand. In her book, *My 1ˢᵗ Book of Questions and Answers,* Carine Mackenzie asks: "What is faith?" The answer: "Faith in Jesus Christ is a gift from God, when we trust in Him completely to save us from sin."[53]

As the sinner is broken by the Law he's spurned, his guilty soul imploring turns to Christ as his only means of reconciliation.[54] He or she abandons every excuse and all hope in self-justification before God and comes to Christ, believes on Christ, unites with Christ, finds Christ lovely, and has full confidence in Christ and His work. The sinner hears the words of Christ revealed in Scripture and believes Him to be his only hope of salvation and sole means of reconciliation with the triune God.[55] That is saving faith.

---

[50] Proverbs 3:5

[51] John 3:16

[52] Charles Spurgeon, *Spurgeon's Sermons*, Vol. 1. (Peabody, MA: Hendrikson, 2011), 370.

[53] Carine Mackenzie, *My 1ˢᵗ Book of Questions and Answers* (Glasgow: Christian Focus, 2011), 42.

[54] From the Hymn *At Calvary.*

[55] John 5:24

Though I joyfully affirm that Christ dwells in the hearts of believers,[56] I deny that the essence of saving faith is articulated well in the command to "ask Jesus to come into your heart." Asking Jesus into your heart is *never* the way the Bible explains saving faith.

Google it. Search a concordance. You'll find that phrase doesn't appear one time in the Bible. If the Bible doesn't explain saving faith that way, why would we try to define saving faith that way?

Faith is running to Jesus as my only hope of righteousness. It acknowledges that there is nothing within me or about me that can demand God's acceptance except Christ alone.

Did you catch that? We need God to *accept us*, not the other way around. In too many evangelistic encounters faith is made out to be me "'accepting' Christ—a term, incidentally, which is not found in the Bible."[57]

Saving faith is a leap into the arms of Christ but it most certainly is not "intellectual suicide," as some would suggest. It is not an irrational jump into the dark, but moving to the light. Faith in Christ is the only rational option there is for all

---

[56] Ephesians 3:17

[57] A.W. Tozer, *The Pursuit of God* (Camp Hill, PA: Christian Publications, 1993). 16. I know that John 1:12 speaks of *receiving* Christ, but this is not the same idea conveyed in many evangelistic encounters where people are told to *accept* Him. True, the New Living Translation translates the word λαμβάνω as "accepted" but this isn't the best sense of the word. Carson notes: "[receiving] faith yields allegiance to the Word, trusts him completely, acknowledges his claims and confesses him with gratitude. That is what it means to 'receive' him," (*The Gospel According to John*, 125-126). This receiving of Christ is the result of being born of God (John 1:13).

humanity and yet many happily rest in the absurdity of their unbelief.[58] Faith is letting go of all human merit and trusting Christ's merit alone.

You weren't more savable because you live in America. You weren't more savable because you tried to be morally good. You were not saved because of Christ *and* anything else. You are saved by, through, and in Christ alone.

Conversely, people aren't *less* savable because of past sin, shame, or rebellion. All stand equally condemned at the foot of the cross because of our lawless deeds. But those who choose Christ alone as their only suitable and all sufficient Savior will find full and free forgiveness and rest for their weary souls.[59]

Saving faith entails a love for the glory of God and a humbling awe at His grace. Saving faith treasures Christ.[60] Saving faith involves a love for Him and for what He has done.[61] Eternal life is *knowing* God personally through Christ.[62] It is an actual relationship with our Savior through faith.

This manifests itself in a life that desires to obey Jesus, love His people, and proclaim the good news of the gospel to others.[63] It is a lifelong seeking of God in Christ. Faith that fizzles, or faith that is fruitless over time, proves to be a faith that

---

[58] See Jeffrey D. Johnson's *The Absurdity of Unbelief* (Conway, AR: Free Grace Press, 2016).

[59] Matthew 11:28-30

[60] Matthew 13:44

[61] 1 Peter 3:8-9

[62] John 17:3

[63] John 14:15, 1 John 3:14, 1 Peter 2:9

was false from the beginning. Saving faith endures to the end.[64] We can be sure of that because God has promised to see us through to the end.[65]

In true saving faith there is a desire to be in Christ, to be with Christ, and to do whatever Christ bids since He is the Shepherd and Overseer of our souls.[66] Saving faith also stirs within us actual longings for Christ.

Faith is not just praying, "come into my heart and be Lord of my life." It's actually wanting God for who He is. It is embracing our chief end: to glorify God and enjoy Him forever. We don't just want God off our backs, but instead want to know Him more, love Him more, serve Him, worship Him, learn about Him, and grow in Him for all eternity.[67]

Finally, saving faith is resting in Christ. It is understanding and trusting that only Christ can bring us to God, not our good works.

It's not Jesus plus what we bring to the table that saves us. It is Christ alone. Sinners must give up trying to appease God and instead run into the arms of Jesus who promises rest for the weary and heavy laden.[68]

Jesus paid it *all.* It is *finished.* As Luther so aptly commented on Galatians 2:11-21, "there is nothing here for us to do. It

[64] John 10:28
[65] Hebrews 13:5
[66] 1 Peter 2:25
[67] See Psalm 111:2 for example.
[68] Matthew 11:28

belongs to us, rather, only to hear these things have been done for us, and by faith grasp hold of them."[69]

We must unwaveringly uphold the truth that, just like repentance, saving faith is a gift of God brought about through the work of the Holy Spirit in the proclamation of the gospel.[70]

Furthermore, it's not a gift we choose to accept any more than we chose to accept the gift of physical life.

Physical life was given to us and as a result we live. Faith is given to us and as a result *we believe.*

We don't choose to accept the gift of faith; we *choose* to believe *because of* the gift of faith. This distinction is crucial to understand. The requirement isn't to have enough faith to accept faith, because "the natural person does not accept the things of the Spirit of God, for they are folly to him, and he is not able to understand them because they are spiritually discerned."[71]

Therefore, the bare necessity is *faith in Christ,* and it is this exact faith that God graciously gives. In no way does this mean that people are passive in their conversion; as though God is dragging people unwillingly to Him who don't really want Him. To the contrary, the faith God gives us enables us to come to Christ.

[69] Lee Gatiss, ed. *Explore by the Book: 90 Days in Genesis, Exodus, Psalms, and Galatians* (Epson, UK: The Good Book Company, 2017), 27.
[70] Ephesians 2:8-9, 2 Timothy 2:25, Acts 11:18, Philippians 1:29
[71] 1 Corinthians 2:14

To become a Christian is to *exercise* the faith that God gives as He draws a person to Himself. A person cannot become a Christian unless they actually come to Jesus.

In talking with an unbeliever, you could discuss it like this: Do you *want* to be saved? You must, as an act of your will, turn to Christ. God will not believe for you. The beautiful thing about this is that God *gives you the will to turn to Him.* A fine line exists between the two truths that God is totally sovereign over salvation, and we are totally responsible. We might not fully understand how that works in tandem, but we know from God's holy word that both things are true.

No one who truly seeks Christ is denied Him.[72] So we can passionately exhort unbelievers to believe on Christ. We must tell them to come to Him now.

We can encourage unbelievers to ask God to help their unbelief so they may draw near to Him through Christ.[73] Any understanding of how salvation works that denies either the necessity of God's sovereign initiative, or the reality of sinners *sincerely choosing* Christ through faith, is deficient.

Faith finds expression when we *confess with our mouth* that Jesus is Lord.[74] This confession Scripture speaks of is a public confession among men. A true believer will confess that Jesus is Lord—not anyone or anything else.

[72] Jeremiah 29:13
[73] Mark 9:24
[74] Romans 10:9

Furthermore, faith expresses itself in calling on the Lord to be saved. "*Whoever* calls on the name of the Lord *will* be saved."[75] No one is saved apart from personally calling on God for salvation.

True faith will cause a sinner to call out to God for mercy in Christ. This is not a formulaic prayer, but a true desire expressed to God to be forgiven of sins and live under the Lordship of Christ. Some cry out to God to save them, when in reality, they do not want the person of God, but merely the promises of heaven.

They go through the motions but for all the wrong reasons. Maybe they cry out because they don't want to go to hell (self-preservation), or because they don't like their current circumstances (jail, poor health), or they want to get a BMW (prosperity gospel), or because someone else is doing it so they want to do it too (peer pressure), or because they like the idea of the community aspect of Christianity and want to feel accepted.

These are a few bad reasons some call out to God for salvation—all while having no real love for Christ. There is no yearning to actually turn from sin. There is no true acknowledgment of Jesus as Lord. Their reasons are as faulty as their profession—and, in time, they are sure to fall away. These are not genuine believers.

Repentance and faith are manifested when people see themselves for who they are and Christ for who He is and they

[75] Romans 10:13, emphasis mine.

turn away from known sin and trust Jesus as their only suitable and all sufficient Savior. There is no canned prayer to recite and no priest is needed, except the High Priest, Christ our Lord, who saves His people from their sins.[76]

While it is true that the terms of repentance and faith are easy to understand, it's equally true that commitment to Christ doesn't necessarily come the first time someone hears the gospel. Faithful men in church history like John Bunyan and David Brainerd have testimonies whereby they struggled with their conversion over a long period of time. This speaks to the reality that sometimes we need to wrestle a little more rather than just check a box and move on.

We must tell lost people to count the cost and consider what God is calling them to do when He commands repentance.[77] They must close with Christ in such a way that they won't give up and walk away a few months or years down the road when things in their life don't work out the way they thought or dreamed they would. They must bow the knee to Jesus in all areas of their life. They must leave no door of their heart locked, giving Jesus the keys to it all.

They must not merely nod their head, or give a thumbs up. Exhort them to run to Christ without reservation in faith. The only type of persons Christ receives are sinners. That's good news since all have sinned and fallen short of the glory of God.[78]

[76] Matthew 1:21
[77] Luke 14:25-34
[78] Romans 3:23

The point of this chapter has been that unbelievers must repent and believe the gospel in order to become Christians. And these graces of repentance and faith must be expressed as demonstrated in Scripture or they are not really *saving* faith and repentance. These are God's terms for becoming a Christian. These are the bare necessities.

Before we close this chapter, let me address baptism because it is so closely tied to faith and repentance in Scripture.[79] David Wells writes:

> The seriousness with which conversion is regarded in the New Testament is revealed by the close relationship between conversion and baptism. In the accounts of group or individual conversion in Acts (three thousand on the day of Pentecost, Acts 2:41; Philip's converts in Samaria, 8:12, Simon, 8:13; the Ethiopian eunuch, 8:35-38; Cornelius, 10:44-48; Lydia, 16:14-15; the Philippian jailer, 16:31-34; Crispus, 18:8; Ephesian believers, 19:1-6) baptism is always specifically mentioned. In each case baptism occurred immediately *after* conversion. This suggests that baptism is intimately associated with the process of conversion as an outward ritual that symbolizes initiation into the Christian life.[80]

In baptism, we trust the promises of God given to us in the gospel and thus it is one *evidence* that we have truly repented and believed the message of Christ. Baptism does not remove

[79] Acts 2:38

[80] David F. Wells, *Turning to God: Reclaiming Christian Conversion as Unique, Necessary, and Supernatural* (Grand Rapids: Baker, 2012), 49. Emphasis mine.

our sin, but is an appeal to God for a good conscience.[81] In this sense, we proclaim our trust in Christ and His work alone, not *our* merits, for the free forgiveness of sins and right standing with God. We aren't trusting the water, but what it signifies, namely the death, burial, and resurrection of Christ.[82] It is a believer's act of obedience once we belong to Him.

Furthermore, baptism symbolizes on the outside what God has done on the inside.[83] Being so closely connected to true repentance and faith, it is the sign God has given us for the New Covenant.

This has led some people to think that baptism is what actually brings about the new birth.[84] But as we've seen above, this is far from scriptural.

God brings about the new birth through the proclamation of His Word whereby the sinner responds in repentance and faith.[85] This is not to diminish the importance of baptism. To the contrary, it is a crucial act of obedience which identifies us publicly with Christ and His people.

A person who refuses baptism may not have fully understood the gospel and its implications.[86] As Jeffrey Johnson has written,

---

[81] See 1 Peter 3:21

[82] Romans 6:4

[83] Titus 3:5

[84] For example, some of Church of Christ and Lutherans believe in Baptismal regeneration.

[85] See another example in Acts 16:14.

[86] I want to be careful here on a few fronts. 1.) I believe my Paedobaptist brothers and sisters are true believers even if they are wrong on this important matter. 2.) In no way am I defending the doctrine that baptism *completes* one's

Although baptism is not essential to salvation, it is highly unlikely that a person has been truly born again without an eager desire to follow the Lord in this first command that God gives the new Christian (Acts 2:38). Baptism is a public confession of Christ (Matt. 10:32-33) that evidences to the church and the world that there has been a radical transformation within. Baptism is also a visible sermon. It demonstrates a spiritual reality of one's death to sin and resurrection to the newness of life in Christ Jesus.[87]

More teaching and instruction may be required before a genuine convert commits to this critical step in the Christian walk. It is not that new believers are *forced* to be baptized. Rather, because of an outpouring of love and gratitude for their Savior, they usually *want* to be baptized—to identify themselves with Christ and His followers.[88]

No person can become a Christian without repentance and faith. These are the bare necessities in our conversion. A person is saved when the gospel is proclaimed and the Spirit works through that proclamation in such a way that He moves the

salvation or is the agent of our regeneration. 3.) I also want to be clear that the *normal* pattern we see in the New Testament is that people were converted and then baptized. We need to be careful we don't make baptism insignificant or "optional."

[87] Jeffrey D. Johnson, *The Church: Her Nature, Authority, Purpose, and Worship*, (New Albany, MS Media Gratiae, 2020), 206.

[88] If they don't embrace baptism then they should be counseled from the Scriptures. It may be they are simply confused, but it also may mean they aren't converted. Again, I'm not talking about a Presbyterian becoming a Baptist. I'm talking about a person who flat out rejects all modes of baptism. That's a problem.

sinner from death to life, turning on the light, so to speak, so that the person sees his or her sin (breaking God's Law) and turns from it in repentance, trusting Christ alone in faith as his or her only suitable and all sufficient Savior.

While this is sufficient for understanding conversion, there are still a few more things that would be helpful for us to consider. We now turn to the precious biblical doctrine of justification.

6

The Great Exchange

"Making a happy exchange with us,
Christ took upon himself our sinful person,
and gave to us his innocent, and victorious person."
Martin Luther[1]

Steve Bartman has a World Series ring. He is the fan who interfered with Chicago Cubs outfielder, Moises Alou, in the 2003 National League Championship Game. I remember watching the replay and seeing Bartman literally put his hand right over the top of Alou's to catch a foul ball, thus depriving the Cubs' defense of a crucial out in Game 6. As a result of this interference, many avid Cubs fans blame Bartman for Chicago's loss to the Florida Marlins, who went on to win the 2003 World Series.

Thirteen years later, the Cubs finally snapped their 108 year drought and won the World Series in a marathon match up against the Cleveland Indians. As a result of this historic victory, Bartman, the interferer, was given a ring. The owner of the Cubs organization said the following about Bartman's ring: "On behalf of the entire Chicago Cubs organization, we are honored to present a 2016 World Series Championship Ring to Mr.

[1] *Explore by the Book*, 35.

Steve Bartman. We hope this provides closure on an unfortunate chapter of the story that has perpetuated throughout our quest to win a long-awaited World Series."[2]

What a gesture indeed! The Chicago Cubs put in countless hours of work, endured the physical toll on their bodies, and persevered through over a century of falling short. It's incredible to think they gave such a token of their crowning achievement to a man who just sat in the stands.

But, he didn't *just* sit in the stands, did he? He *prevented* the Cubs from breaking the World Series drought 13 years earlier! But now, Steve Bartman, of all people, has a World Series ring.

Of course, no one looks at Mr. Bartman as if *he* actually won the World Series just because he has the hardware. His name won't be written in any record books. His jersey won't be retired. All he did was receive a ring from a generous organization.

Sure, it's a valuable a ring, and the 2016 World Series was certainly a contest that won't soon be forgotten, but that doesn't have any bearing on who *Bartman* is. In fact, even with this ring, many will forever remember him as that guy who robbed the Cubs of their rings in 2003. The ring hasn't changed his *identity*. Having a ring doesn't make him a member of the Cubs.

Sadly, too many understand salvation in this same sense. Jesus did something great, and lets us in on it, but it doesn't really have any bearing on who *we* are. We still think of

[2]   Story from: https://www.si.com/mlb/2017/07/31/steve-bartman-cubs-world-series-ring

ourselves as just "ole sinners" moping around. We think we are the same as we used to be, but now at least we have a ring.

The Bible does not describe Christians in this way. Believers are referred to throughout the New Testament as *saints.*[3] Because of our confusion about a Christian's standing in Christ, it is important for us to spend a chapter on justification. We desperately need to recover this important doctrine.

How does salvation work? Gospel proclamation, God's initiating work, personal faith and repentance, and now we see the crucial aspect of justification.

Step Four: God Justifies the Sinner

What exactly is justification?

First, let's address the *when* instead of the *what.* Justification does not happen until a person comes to Christ in faith.[4] No one has peace with God unless they repent and believe the gospel. If nothing changes they will meet God in judgment—and then eternal punishment.

This is important to clarify because although the work of Christ is effectual for His people, it is not applied until a moment in time. You can't walk around saying that the death of Jesus is good news for you if you never place your faith in Christ

[3] See Philippians 1:1. This word is used over 60x in the New Testament to refer to Believers.

[4] We are justified by faith alone. And remember, the faith that saves is a faith that *repents.*

and turn from your sin. Justification doesn't occur until the moment in time that one places his faith in Christ.

There's the *when.* How about the *what?*

The Baptist Faith and Message says, "Justification is God's gracious and full acquittal upon principles of His righteousness of all sinners who repent and believe in Christ. Justification brings the believer unto a relationship of peace and favor with God."[5]

When a sinner places his faith in Christ, he has peace with God and is clothed in the righteous robes of Jesus.[6] To use an old play on words, "justified" is "just as if I'd" always obeyed God perfectly. Justification is a legal declaration by which God credits the sinner with all the perfect work Jesus did because, on the cross, Jesus was credited with all the evil he or she did.[7]

That is how God responds to us.[8] He declares us righteous based on the merit of Christ alone through the very faith He has gifted to us. When we trust Christ, God declares us forever justified; not because our *faith* is righteous, but because the object of our faith, Christ, is righteous.[9]

The righteousness of Christ is *imputed* to us by faith because on the cross our sins were imputed to Him. A great exchange indeed.

---

[5] *Baptist Faith and Message* (2000), Heading IV, B.

[6] Romans 5:1, 2 Corinthians 5:21

[7] Isaiah 53:6

[8] Of course, we see God's response is based on His prior initiative, isn't it? Salvation is all of grace from beginning to end!

[9] Philippians 3:9

Therefore, justification is a one-time act and it is and has *always* been received by grace alone through faith alone in Christ alone.[10] Once a person is justified they are always justified.[11] They are declared righteous by God through Christ and in the eyes of God that never changes. The sinner is forgiven of all sins past, present, and future, and given such a high status that he or she can boldly enter the throne room of God.[12]

Furthermore, the Christian does not have to await some future justification, hoping that he has done enough to maintain his status before God. All those justified will be glorified – case closed.[13]

None of this is because of our own work, or what we've done or failed to do, or how good we try to be. It is all because of God's mercy in Christ.[14]

The requirement to stand before a Holy God is perfect righteousness. And this is exactly what has been secured for us by the work of Christ. The very perfection God demands of us is the same perfection He graciously gives to us in Christ.

> *Clothed in His righteousness alone,*
> *Faultless to stand before the Throne.*[15]

No words can describe this astonishing truth with the praise and gratitude it deserves. The magnanimity of God in Christ to

[10] Genesis 15:6
[11] Romans 8:29-30
[12] Hebrews 4:16
[13] Romans 8:30
[14] Titus 3:7
[15] The hymn, *My Hope is Built* by Edward Mote.

take upon Himself the wrath we deserve and to freely bestow His *righteousness* upon us seems too good to be true until we realize it's not.

This great exchange is the burning core of the gospel. The goal of Christ's work in salvation was not that we could start afresh and *become* righteous by our own deeds. *None* of us would make it.

Instead, He gives us *His* righteousness, received by faith.[16] We are *not* justified because of our faith *and* subsequent lifestyle. We are *not* justified by faith *and* baptism, the Lord's Supper, or how much we read the Bible.

We are justified based on the work and merit of Jesus, *alone.* This isn't Jesus giving us a World Series ring and leaving us as mere fans in the stands. This is Jesus changing our status before God. We do not possess the paraphernalia of salvation like fanboys, but are actually *united* to Christ.

Just because you have a World Series ring doesn't mean anyone in their right mind will look at you like they do Kris Bryant. Yet, in justification God sees Christ in me. I am in Christ and He is in me. I have union with Him. All that Jesus accomplished for me is truly, actually, and really mine by faith. Legally, it's just as if I had always perfectly obeyed God. My sin is Christ's and His righteousness is mine. What a great exchange!

There is no assurance of salvation any other way. If your assurance of salvation comes from Jesus *and* anything else, you

[16] 2 Corinthians 5:21

will always be left wondering if you are doing good enough to get into heaven.

Does faith in Christ result in a changed lifestyle? Absolutely. But if you say, "I know I'm saved because I'm doing all of this stuff," let me caution you. If you believe your works will result in eternal salvation, you are sadly mistaken. Don't be the one to whom Jesus said, "Depart from me. I never knew you."

Christians will always struggle with sin in the present world, whether that be by not loving God as much as we should, loving ourselves too much, not loving our neighbors as we should, giving with impure motivations, imperfections in our repentance, or any number of other things.[17] In this life, we are always lacking in some area. There is always something that God has told us to do that we aren't doing well or something God has told us not to do that we find ourselves doing. We are still plagued with sins of omission and sins of commission. And if we are honest, it's often in many areas. As Luther said, Christians are simultaneously justified, yet also sinners.[18]

This is why the gospel promise of justification by faith alone is our only steadfast anchor for assurance of salvation. It is the pillow on which we may lay our heads in sweet gospel comfort. Christ has seen my worst and He owned my sin anyway. He has seen all of my half-hearted efforts, my carelessness with His truth, my failures, mistakes, and the heinousness of all my sin. But on the cross He said *mine*, anyway. He became God-

---

[17] 1 John 1:8

[18] Luther's famous phrase "*Simul justus et peccator.*"

forsaken so that I would not be forsaken by God. "Gospel-comfort springs from a gospel-root, which is Christ."[19]

This means that in Christ, God is for us. God isn't out to get us. There aren't a few drops of wrath left that we need to take upon ourselves. We are just as justified a millisecond after we receive Christ as we will be at the end of our life. It's a once for all justification.

We don't get a flat tire because we didn't put enough money in the offering plate on Sunday. When I wake up in the morning and snap at my wife or kids, I'm still justified. When I get up and spend an hour in prayer, I'm still just as justified as before (no *bonus* justification). When I forget to or don't want to pray, I'm still justified. This is because *none* of justification is based on what I do, but on what Jesus has already completed for me.

When we sin, we are essentially telling Jesus to turn back and depart from us like Naomi said to her daughters-in-law. But Christ is like Ruth ever clinging to us and committing Himself to be with us even to our death.[20] He is not letting go of His Bride.[21]

We must stop thinking of God as a Zeus in the sky who eagerly anticipates our next display of stupidity so He can strike us with a lightning bolt. We must stop thinking of God as merely tolerating our existence. God doesn't treat us like we treat our third cousin whom we say we love but can't stand being around.

---

[19] *Christian in Complete Armour*, 1:218.
[20] Ruth 1:11-18
[21] Ephesians 5:31-32

He doesn't just want to be around us once a year at the obligatory family holiday celebrations.

God enjoys Christians. He delights in us. Scripture tells us He sings *loudly* over us![22] We *know* God loves us because of the lengths He went to in rescuing us from our sins and bringing us back to Himself. Our standing with Him is high and this is not because we've earned it. It's because of what Christ has done in our place. By faith, we are clothed in His righteousness. God is *for us* in Christ!

I mention justification in this book because it is so misunderstood by many in our society today, even faithful Christians. Many believe that God is in heaven, anxious for us to mess up so He can teach us a lesson. He's given us the World Series ring but if we don't live up to His demands, He's ready to take it back in the blink of an eye. He has us on the team, but He really hopes we never have to get in the game because He knows we'll just mess up the whole thing. When we strike out for the thousandth time, we are convinced God must think we are idiots and really doesn't want anything more to do with us. This is a gross misunderstanding of the gospel.

Christ is the believer's substitute and legal representative. He became a curse so that we could have fellowship with God.[23] When Jesus bore our sins in His body on the tree, He did so in such a way as to fully, finally, and completely exhaust every ounce of God's wrath against us.[24]

[22] Zephaniah 3:17
[23] Galatians 3:13
[24] 1 Peter 2:24

Full justification is applied to us when we come to Christ in saving faith. Yes, we do still face consequences for sin in this life, but there is no longer any condemnation for us from God.[25] Literally, none. Zero. Zip. Zilch. Nada. Jesus has taken care of it all. We can only lose our justification if Christ can lose His righteousness. That's not happening.

Christians were once alienated from God, but that is no longer the case.[26] The wrath of God for our sin is all gone. It has been propitiated by Christ.[27] Christ drank the foaming cup of the wrath of God down to the last dreg and there's nothing left in that cup for you to drink, so keep drinking from the rivers of grace.

Believers aren't going to meet Christ face to face one day and have Him say, "Ah, boy. I guess you can come in, but you'll need to find a seat somewhere in the back." Instead, Jesus will warmly say to all Christians, "Come, you who are blessed by my Father; inherit the kingdom prepared for you from the foundation of the world."[28]

Perhaps I can illustrate this more clearly with the concept of résumés. For thousands of years the human race somehow existed without these headaches. If you've ever had to write one, or go through an endless stack of them looking for the perfect

---

[25] Romans 8:1

[26] Colossians 1:21

[27] I know that "propitiation" is a big word! But we need to recover it in our vocabulary. Propitiation is a "wrath satisfying sacrifice". See Romans 3:25 and 1 John 2:2.

[28] Matthew 25:34

employee, then you know exactly what I'm talking about. And yet, in our day, they have become a necessary evil.

They can make the difference between a quality, high paying job, and one that barely makes ends meet. I wonder, given the opportunity before God, what you might want to put on your spiritual résumé.

If you were applying for acceptance into heaven, what kind of qualifications do you have to get there? Maybe God is looking for someone with sufficient experience in doing good deeds? Or maybe He prefers a person who hasn't had too many mess ups?

Is your education enough? Can you analyze Greek and Hebrew sentences? Does your lack of education disqualify you? Do you have enough volunteer hours?

If God gave an entrance exam, could you pass it? Does your extra tithing help curve the grade? The truth is, the only résumés accepted in heaven are those containing just one word. What word? Follow with me here for a moment.

There are essentially three kinds of people when it comes to our hypothetical spiritual résumés:

1. "I sin. A lot! You wouldn't believe all the stuff I've done. But so what?" These are the ones who can write a book about all of their sin and wickedness. They sin, and don't care. What will God do with these résumés and the people who've written them? They will be discarded forever.

2. "God's pretty lucky to have me!" These people know they're not perfect . . . but they're pretty close. Their resume is filled with what they do for the Lord—and they're proud of it. They

hope the good they do outweighs the bad, but their behavior and attitude is the standard—not God's word. What happens to their résumés? They go in the discard pile as well. Anyone who relies on their own good works has no hope of entering heaven.

3. "Christ." One word. And that one word is all-encompassing. These people know that they do not deserve heaven. They do not deserve the grace and love of the Father. But they also understand that He gave it to them anyway. It is not because of their own works that they will see eternity with Christ—it's because of His! This is the only résumé He accepts.

This third kind of person is who we are, if we genuinely belong to the King. All our evil deeds, all our wicked thoughts, all our breaking of God's Holy Law, all our lack of kindness toward others, all of our hateful words, all of our sin, shame, guilt, and sorrow has been dealt with on the cross.

He took our résumés, marked out our name, and wrote His own in blood across the top. He who committed no sin, bore ours. The Righteous One was treated as unrighteous.[29] In our place, condemned, He stood. He bore the legal penalty for our sins against God. Therefore, for all the sins mentioned above and countless others I can put just one word: *Christ.* This is justification. My résumé has been replaced with Christ's.

All of my "good" deeds—my church attendance, financial contributions, Bible reading and knowledge, leadership in my family—I am only enabled to do these things because of Christ's

[29] 1 Peter 3:18

mercy, and even in them my motivations are not quite pure. My zeal isn't fervent enough, my love isn't lovely enough, and my worship isn't honoring enough. There is enough sin remaining even in these good things to warrant my condemnation, and yet, in all of this, just one word says it all: *Christ.*

The worst that I am isn't beyond the blood of Jesus. The best that I am isn't beyond the blood of Jesus. All I have to claim before God is the work of His Son on my behalf. Hallelujah! All I have is Christ! And He is enough. And by faith, I receive Christ and all of His benefits. I am justified. Just as if I'd always done perfectly before God as Jesus did. All I have to claim on my spiritual résumé is Christ, and that is precisely what (Who!) God joyfully accepts.

Christians are accepted by God in Christ. Is there any better news in the entire universe? This is justification by faith alone—the greatest exchange in the history of the world.

When I wake up tomorrow and don't feel like a pastor, God accepts me in Christ. When I am not the parent I need to be, God accepts me in Christ. Whether you like or don't like this book, God accepts me in Christ. When I preach "a home-run" sermon, God doesn't love me more. When I strike out, or hit into a double play, God doesn't love me less. When I read the Bible hungry for more of God, I am holy loved and loved wholly. When I read the Bible fearful of its conviction, I am holy loved and loved wholly. I am accepted in Christ, clothed in His righteousness, all by faith alone.

Having only one word on my spiritual résumé leaves it almost blank as far as paper goes. No work experience. No volunteer hours. No education. No awards. No accolades. No letters behind my name. But just because it is almost blank doesn't mean it's empty. That one word speaks eternally for me. All of His righteous deeds are mine. His atoning death is mine. All I have is Christ.

If you are a believer, take a moment to let this sink in. All you have is Christ, and that's the most glorious news in the universe. You have Him by faith. He looks at you and says "Mine! Here is a blood bought rebel washed in My blood and clothed in My righteousness! And I love him like my Father loves Me."

Believer, you have a spotless résumé, impeccable work experience, and not an ounce of sin to pay for—because you have been forgiven in Jesus—cleansed and declared righteous. This completely obliterates the prosperity gospel. When we truly understand what it means to be justified by faith alone, it makes getting earthly health and worldly wealth seem like refuse compared to Christ. Jesus is the treasure.

That's what Paul says in Philippians 3:7-9. This reality ought also to obliterate any sort of scheming we might come up with to *attract* people to church. How do you put the good news of justification by faith alone on the same playing field as free t-shirts?

What we are offered in the gospel is the most astounding news in the universe. It's not a ring. It's not a new nametag.

What we are offered in the gospel is full and complete pardon of all sins, and the righteousness of Christ, all so that we can be brought into full fellowship with the triune God.[30] "We are saved from God to God by God through God for God. The godhead works in concert so that salvation will engulf you in God."[31]

Do you realize just how remarkable that is?

If you are a believer, this *is* your reality. Make it a daily habit to focus on the gospel so that you can constantly remind yourself of your standing with God in Christ.

What about unbelievers? They too can have Christ and His righteousness. We must explain to them that the question is not whether they *can* have Him, but whether they actually *want* Him.

Will they have Him? No one who wants Christ is turned away from Him. We must urge them to come to Him in faith; to repent and believe the gospel without delay.

We could ask them questions like: Will you trust His atoning blood as the only possible payment for your sin? Will you, by faith, trust that His righteousness is the only thing that can prepare you for a perfect eternity in the presence of God and His people forever? Will you repent, in your heart turning from your love of sin, and come to Christ in faith as your only suitable and all sufficient Savior? Will you lay aside any hope that you have in your own merit?

When a sinner comes to Christ in faith, the good news of justification is his forever. You might say, "I thought you said

[30] John 17:21
[31] *Gospel Deeps*, 75.

God had to initiate the response!" I did say that. And I stand by it. Whether it *feels* like it or not, if it's one's desire to come to Christ, God has already initiated this transaction. Our love for Christ is in response to His love for us.

How does salvation work? The gospel is proclaimed, and God initiates a response. Then, the sinner comes to Christ in saving faith, repenting of his sin against a Holy God. As a result of our faith in Christ alone, God declares us forever justified before Him. Jesus did a perfect work and as a result, Christians are treated by God just as if we'd always obeyed Him perfectly.

Shai Linne sums up what I've said thus far beautifully on his album *Still Jesus:*

> All of my inconsistencies, All of my idiosyncrasies
> Still, you pursue relentlessly
> At times, I wonder how this can be
> Surely, it's because of the cross
> Where Jesus paid the full penalty
> And bore the burden of sin's great cost
> I'm saved by grace through faith in God
> I look to Christ and I trust He died
> So even though I'm being sanctified
> I can't be any more justified
> His work is finished, that cannot change
> And with this knowledge, I am free
> Forever there's grace and will remain
> Because of what happened at Calvary[32]

[32] Shai Linne's song *Immutable* from the Album *Still Jesus.* Lamp Mode Records, 2017.

This might make a good stopping place. But because of the number of walking dead, we should examine one final aspect of salvation before we are finished.

Those who by faith alone are legally counted as though they have obeyed because of the merit of Jesus, in turn seek to live a life of obedience in Him. We turn now to the ongoing, lifelong process of *sanctification.*

7

Living Things Grow

*"Sanctification is the real change in man from the sordidness
of sin to the purity of God's image."*
—William Ames[1]

My wife and I have been blessed with five beautiful children. It has been an amazing grace of God in our lives to see these babies grow up. Our oldest has gone from not being able to hold his head up to begging us to play full pads football this year. Our baby is in the smiling, sitting up, and reaching stage right now when it seems like just yesterday we just found out my wife was pregnant with him.

That's one of the things kids do best, isn't it? *Grow.* If children don't get bigger and brighter year by year that signals a substantial problem. It's not only their physical stature that changes though. They go from liking Dora to Ninja Turtles; from baby food to Pop-Tarts; from nursery rhymes to Kidz Bop. It is perfectly natural to see almost daily changes in the life of a child.

Alden T. Vaughan, *The Puritan Tradition in America: 1620-1730* (Hanover, NH: University Press of New England, 1972), 19.

Step Five: Sanctification

This serves as a wonderful analogy to the doctrine of sanctification. When a person moves from death to life, they grow.[2] Sometimes this growth is perceptible on a daily basis, and sometimes it's mainly noticeable over a longer period of time. They are now part of the realm of spiritual life, and *living things grow.* Spiritual maturity results from the biblical process known as *sanctification.*

The word *sanctify* comes from the word *holy.* Quite literally, sanctification is being made *holy* – set apart by God and conformed to the image of Christ. We live out the realities of our salvation as God works in us to bring about practical holiness in our lives.[3]

Wayne Grudem defines sanctification as, "a progressive work of God and man that makes us more and more free from sin and more like Christ in our actual lives."[4] True believers live a life of dying to sin and living to righteousness.[5] There are many other wonderful aspects of our salvation I could have included in this book, but I include this doctrine of sanctification for a pointed purpose.[6]

The goal of this chapter is to demonstrate the absolute necessity of progressive sanctification if one has passed from

---

[2] 2 Peter 3:18

[3] Philippians 2:12-13

[4] Wayne Grudem, *Systematic Theology: An Introduction to Biblical Doctrine* (Grand Rapids: Zondervan, 1994), 1254.

[5] 1 Peter 2:24

[6] Such as our adoption or future glorification.

death to life. Just like we do not remain babies forever, a true believer does not remain a spiritual infant either. A person's profession of faith is in question if there is zero growth in Jesus over the course his life.[7] "Repentance that is not ongoing is not genuine; faith that does not involve surrender is not adequate; a life in which holiness does not develop is not Christian."[8]

You might be thinking, "But wait a second! I thought we were *already* counted righteous in Christ by faith alone!" Unquestionably, we are, and that legal declaration will never change.

Yet, there's another aspect we should consider. True believers are made holy by the power of God. The work of Christ didn't merely purchase a legal declaration, but also the practical application of holiness. How marvelous are the blessings that flow to Christians because of Christ's work! This is another blessing the believer possesses in Jesus.

J.C. Ryle elaborates:

The Lord Jesus has undertaken everything that His people's souls require: not only to deliver them from the guilt of their sins by His atoning death, but from the dominion of their sins, by placing in their hearts the Holy Spirit; not only to justify them, but also to sanctify them.[9]

---

[7] It's not that they *were* a Christian but now aren't. Rather, they never were a Christian at all (1 John 2:19).

[8] *Because We Love Him*, 13.

[9] *Holiness*, 16.

Christ's work on the cross actually sets captives free so we can die to sin and live to righteousness.[10] Because of grace, we are no longer slaves to sin. Once we are set free our desires change. We no longer live to sin, but we want to live our lives for the glory of God.[11]

His sheep hear His voice and *follow* Him.[12] Choosing righteousness as a Christian isn't being a Pharisee. It is being a Christian.[13] It reminds me of the Geico© commercials currently airing: "If you're a cat, you ignore people. It's what you do."[14] Well, if you're a Christian, you love to follow Jesus. It's what you do. It is what we do because of who we now are.

The Bible teaches that if we truly love Christ, we obey His commands. If we do not obey Him, yet say we love Him, the Bible says we are liars and the truth is not in us. Strong language for a strong message. If we love Him, we follow Him—not perfectly, of course, but that is our desire. The awesome reality of justification doesn't create believers who care nothing about holiness, but instead produces Christians who strive after it.[15]

Sanctification is an ongoing process and it takes place throughout the entirety of a Christian's life. We never reach perfection here but are made more and more into the image of Christ.[16]

---

[10] 1 Peter 2:24
[11] Romans 6:1-2
[12] John 10:27
[13] 1 John 3:10
[14] http://www.ispottv/ad/7mXj/geico-go-get-help-its-what-you-do
[15] Hebrews 12:14
[16] Philippians 1:6, Romans 8:29

The Holy Spirit now dwells within those who belong to the Lord.[17] That indwelling carries with it numerous blessings, but one of those is that we truly and actually grow in holiness.[18] He works in us "both to will and to work for His good pleasure."[19]

The Apostle Peter says that Christians are to sanctify the Lord in our hearts, meaning that we set Him apart as Holy.[20] This changes us. We fight sin. We pursue holiness. We follow Christ as Lord. We come to love His people, and gather regularly and routinely with the local church.

These blessings were secured for us in the work of Christ on the cross and were applied to us when we were converted. The Holy Spirit works in us to bring these blessings to fruition—gifting us, convicting us, illuminating the Word to us, and holding Christ before us as glorious.

Another reason to include sanctification in a book about how salvation works is because no one can see justification, but certain aspects of sanctification are visible. We can't see the wind but we know it's blowing because the trees are moving. We can't see the Holy Spirit moving but we can see His fruit in the lives of saints who have called upon Christ for salvation.[21]

Sanctification begins immediately upon a person's conversion to Christ. It doesn't take a few years to "kick in" and it never "kicks out." Immediately, through the work of the Spirit,

---

[17] Romans 8:12-17
[18] Ephesians 1:3, 1 Peter 1:13-16, 1 John 3:6-7
[19] Philippians 2:13
[20] 1 Peter 3:15
[21] John 3:8, Galatians 5:22

the new believer is given new desires, new hopes, new affections, new tastes, and new loves. This newness is acted upon by the will. No, not all of this is mature at first, but all of it is present and will continue to grow. It all results from God's endless supply of grace.

In too many evangelistic scenarios a person is asked to repeat a prayer. That's usually followed by asking whether or not he really meant it. If he gives an affirmative answer, sometimes he is called before the church and subsequently baptized without any evidence of this changed condition in Christ.

It would be wiser, and more consistent with a Baptist understanding of regenerate church membership, to wait until that evidence emerges before stepping into the waters of baptism. No one can judge the heart. But we can see the fruit of regeneration displayed in our sanctification. And we can also see the lack of it.[22]

Professing Christ as Lord and Savior is obviously important, but that in and of itself does not mean a sinner has truly been born again. Jesus says loving Him is doing what He bids us to do.[23]

Remember, some make professions they honestly do not mean. If this were not so, everyone who makes a profession of faith would remain in Christ forever. Sadly, plenty seem afire with Christ—but after a little time has gone by, they return to

---

[22] I'm not suggesting a year long wait period, but sufficient counsel in conjunction with life observation for new converts. This is especially important in areas like the Bible-Belt where Christianity has become cultural.

[23] John 14:15, Luke 6:46

their old ways with rarely a thought of the One they confessed to love.

My heart breaks as I think of a person right now who professed Christ last year but has recently gone back into the world. It is my hope that he is a true Christian who has momentarily succumbed to sin. But it is also possible he has proven himself to never have truly been converted. Time will tell.

As we discussed above, a true believer follows Christ's commands and bears spiritual fruit. If one says he or she loves Jesus but incessantly refuses to give up known sin, it's likely his claim is false.

A person who says "I know what I need to do," but never strives to do it (even imperfectly) doesn't really love Jesus.[24] An intellectual acknowledgement of the facts of the gospel followed by a verbal profession of said acknowledgment doesn't guarantee that a person has passed from death to life.[25]

Believers are not a kitchen remodel. They are an entirely new house. This is why the Bible describes us as a *new* creation.[26] Everything changes.

In our joy at receiving additional converts for the Lord, many times we forget to caution them about the reality of false conversions. Sadly, some pastors go as far as telling them to stamp a date in a Bible and never question anything about

[24] James 4:17, Hebrews 12:14
[25] James 2:19
[26] 2 Corinthians 5:17

salvation ever again. They are told, "Don't let anyone ever tell you any different—that's just Satan trying to make you doubt."

This sad situation has kept many from the important self-examination we, as believers, regularly perform.[27] In the Bible, we're told to examine our lives, to make sure of our calling, and to work out our salvation.[28] It should alarm us if we do not ever see evidence of fruit and regular, continual repentance in our lives.

Yes, we repent when we initially come to Christ. But sin doesn't stop there. As long as we sin, we are called to repent and live a lifestyle of repentance toward God and faith in Christ. Sanctification is a lifelong process.

Thankfully, sometimes these who make false professions of faith encounter the gospel later in life and, by God's grace, make a real and true confession of Christ as Lord and Savior. Sadly, too many refuse to ever consider their lives and continue living in sin while clinging to the false hope of their name written on a church roll somewhere.

Affections, Actions, and Attitudes

Here's a helpful alliteration to assist in discerning whether or not the gospel has actually taken root in a person's heart: *affections*, *actions*, and *attitudes*. Essentially, all the ways that sin has left us

---

[27] We cannot let the precious doctrine of eternal security mean every person who ever gives a hat tip to Jesus will go to heaven.

[28] 2 Peter 1:10, Philippians 2:12

totally depraved, the gospel comes in and begins to affect and rearrange.

First, if the gospel has taken root, a person's affections will be changed.[29] The truth of the gospel enters the mind and affects the heart. Affections, more than mere emotion, are better understood as deeply rooted longings.

Our affections are what we really *want.* If Christ reigns in our hearts, it means we'll desire Him. Believers can be characterized as people who love Christ with a deep-seated love.

Christians desire Christ as our supreme treasure. We aren't satisfied with the Sunday morning small talk of football games, hunting, and the latest sale prices. We long to talk about Christ with one another because we truly love Him.

Furthermore, an increasing love for Christ goes hand in hand with a decreasing interest in the things the world has to offer us.[30] As we grow in Christ we become less and less enamored with the accolades and applause of men. Even what society might consider *good things,* we may choose to cast away if they hinder our worship of the One whom our soul loves.[31]

Secondly, as previously discussed, our actions change. When the gospel penetrates our hearts and changes our affections for Christ it will show in our outward behavior.

Show me a person who loves football, and I'll show you a person who enjoys going to football games. Show me a person

[29] Deuteronomy 30:6
[30] 1 John 2:15-17
[31] Hebrews 12:1 (Song of Solomon 3:4)

in love with Christ and I will show you a person who is zealous for good works and seeking to live righteously.

It is contradictory for a person to say, "I love Jesus," but simultaneously live their life apart from what Christ commands. Phrases like, "I love Jesus, but not the church," "I love Jesus, but don't have time for the Bible," or, "I love Jesus, but I don't want to be considered as 'holier than thou' or come across as legalistic," hold no water when examined in light of the New Testament.

They make as much sense as a person who says, "Apple is the best company ever," but he doesn't know what an iPhone is. If I tell you, "I love spinach," you would probably cook me some when I visit your house for supper. You could reasonably expect that when I took a bite I would love it. If I curled up my nose, instead of diving right in, and said, "What is this green stuff? It looks terrible!" you might question my truthfulness. A disconnect exists when we profess our love for something—anything—but never show that profession to be true by our actions.

In this way, when someone says they love Jesus, we have a biblical expectation that their actions will match their profession over time. We have a reasonable and biblical expectation that they will love Scripture, the local church, righteous living, prayer, generosity, and God's people as well as being engaged in hating sin. So if we hear a profession of faith in Christ, but don't see the fruit or evidence of that profession, we begin to question their commitment and/or honesty.[32]

That's because those who have received the decree of "no condemnation" *for* sin have no desire for compromise *with* sin.[33] Instead, believers *want* to obey Jesus because they love Him.[34]

This means we can't use the excuse of, "that's just the way I am," to continue in sin, whether we are trying to justify greed, anger, homosexuality, or a litany of other sins. If we are believers, that's not who we are any more. It's who we *were.*[35] *Now* is a new day. Now we *put on* the things of Christ because we have been *transformed* by the power of the gospel.[36]

No, this is not perfectionism. None of us will ever come anywhere close to perfection. That's why we need Christ's finished work. The reality of the gospel is that it truly is the power of God to bring people from *death to life.*

As Davies preached: "It does not appear a kind of privilege to the true penitent that he cannot be perfect in this life, but it is the daily burden and grief of his soul that he is not."[37] Christians

---

[32] For example, John says, " *We know* that we have passed *out of death into life, because* we love the brothers," (1 John 3:14, emphasis mine). Love for the local church is an indicator that a person is a believer. A lack of love for the Body indicates that someone is *not* a true believer. A commitment to the local church does not *guarantee* one is committed to Christ. But lack of meaningful commitment to the local church reveals a serious issue and may in fact indicate that one is not actually a Christian.

[33] Romans 8:1-13

[34] John 14:15

[35] 1 Corinthians 6:11

[36] Colossians 3:12ff, Romans 12:1-2.

[37] *Salvation In Full Color*, 209.

desire, in increasing measure, to be ever freer from sin and have all areas of their lives under Christ's kingship. Believers want to be more like Him. Living things grow.

Thirdly, the gospel affects our attitudes. The motivation behind our actions is the glory of God. If the gospel has taken root in my heart, then it is my desire to bring Him glory in all that I do.

It is not my desire to merely "do enough to get by" but to do *all I can* to bring God glory in my worship—giving, serving, and living. My motivation for life becomes glorifying God and enjoying Him forever.[38] The glory of God is the end goal in all things for the Christian.

A gospel shaped attitude is what enables us to live in harmony with the local church. Sister Nona likes to sing slightly off key. Brother Bryce is a little eccentric in his mannerisms. The team working with children did not pick the theme for Vacation Bible School that I would have chosen. But I patiently love them all because my motivation is to see Christ glorified in the unity of His church.

Conversion to Christ occurs instantaneously. If that conversion is genuine, we will be able to see changes in that person. If it's not, we won't.

No, we can't play Holy Spirit and know what's in the heart of man. But we can use the discernment He gives us to see

---

[38] 1 Corinthians 10:31

evidence of such a dramatic event as conversion—still the greatest miracle in one person's life.

We *rejoice* when someone professes Christ as Lord and Savior. Then, even as we hope to teach and encourage and support that new believer, we also know we should be able to see the difference wrought in his heart.[39]

This is messy at times because God saves *sinners.* Sinners always carry baggage. We must be patient with new believers as God works in them. You didn't get to where you are today overnight, did you? And you and I *still* aren't where we need to be. So, patience and genuine love are a necessity with new brothers and sisters in the faith.[40]

This being said, the reality remains: not everyone who *professes* Jesus as Lord and Savior will prove their profession to be genuine. As we've previously discussed, sometimes people "make a decision for Christ" for varied reasons—sometimes because of wrong motives and other times because of a temporary attraction to the Lord that flutters out of existence two days later. If that happens, that decision was not genuine.

Sometimes conversion is a dramatic event—maybe not as dramatic as that of Paul on the road to Damascus—but one we remember forever. Sometimes conversion *appears* to take place

---

[39] Jesus teaches that over time the good soil will produce good fruit. I don't think He means that only 1 in 4 people who hear the gospel will become Christian, but I do think we must listen to our King as He speaks both authoritatively and wisely on this matter. See Matthew 13:1-9, 18-23.

[40] 1 Corinthians 13

gradually.[41] We may not fully know the exact moment of salvation.

I am not suggesting that people are getting saved apart from the proclamation of the gospel or personal repentance and faith—this is impossible.[42] What I mean is that Scripture makes less out of when conversion happened and more out of the fact that it *did* happen.

And if it happened, the fruits of sanctification will show. Are the affections, actions, and attitudes changed? When the New Testament writers exhort readers to examine their salvation they aren't telling people to think back to the moment of conversion but rather asking them to consider if they love Christ *now*.[43] Is there fruit in their life *now*?[44] Is there obedience *now*?

Can we lose our salvation? Absolutely not. Not if that profession was genuine. Spiritually speaking, there is no such thing as going from death to life and then back to death. But if that profession was genuine, spiritual fruit *will* show in our lives— even if, at times, that fruit may appear weak or almost non-existent.

The fires of salvation sometimes appear as warm embers. Then again, we may experience seasons in our lives where, spiritually, we feel like Tom Hanks on *Castaway,* who just lost his Wilson. Often though, God gives us blessed periods where

[41] Conversion is instantaneous in conjunction with regeneration. This does not mean we can always accurately pinpoint it. Not everyone knows for sure when their first birth took place. But they do know they're alive, don't they?

[42] See chapter 2 and 4.

[43] 2 Peter 1:10, 2 Corinthians 13:5, 1 John 5:13

[44] Galatians 5:22

those slow burning embers fan into flame and burn hot with zeal and fervor for the Lord and His kingdom! Ah, what a joy that is.

Because the Holy Spirit is within us and because Christ bled for us and rose again, we are not left to ourselves to ultimately fall away. We *will* bear fruit. It's a gospel promise.[45]

His grace provides the fuel for us to live for Him and is the very source for the fruit we bear. God doesn't leave us to bear fruit through our own power but works in us daily.

If you've been beaten up and broken down in your Christian walk lately, know that His sanctifying grace can bandage all wounds, and replenish your desires for Christ. He never gives up on His own. Go to Him daily, for His mercies are new every morning.[46] Once He's redeemed you, He will see you through to the end—maturing you in Himself along the way.

In short, when we struggle with assurance of salvation, we don't need to look for the date of our conversion as much as we need to look to Christ and His completed work now. As I look to Jesus, I will see in my life signs and evidences of the spiritual fruit that is reflective of a life in Christ. Sometimes those evidences may be hard to personally perceive, but God has given us the local church help us see them.

"Sanctification is the evidence of reconciliation, proving that faith has truly apprehended Christ."[47] Living things grow. All

[45] John 15:5
[46] Lamentations 3:23
[47] *Valley of Vision*, 103.

believers have struggles and failings, but at the same time, Christ's work has secured for Himself a people zealous for good works.[48]

Therefore, when we acknowledge a profession of faith, we rejoice, but we also lovingly, patiently, and graciously watch. It's important that we discern the Lord's working in that new life. And we discern that by the evidences of conversion wrought by the Spirit, not mere intellectual ascent to the facts of the gospel, before we pronounce people as believers and admit them to the baptismal waters.

Again, this isn't to be thought of as an interrogation or that we need to see perfection, for none of us would meet that standard. But we should be able to see true change when one passes from death to life.

Is this *judgmental?* In a way, yes. But not in the condemning sense. Rather, it is judging in the way that Christ has called His church to judge, with discernment. Don't buy into the lie that making a judgment is wrong.

We make judgments all the time. We choose this place to eat over that one. We judge which clothes to wear based on the temperature outside. So, we don't condemn people to hell or grant them entrance to heaven. We don't have that power. But we do have the responsibility to think about the authenticity of a person's conversion based on the evidences we have before

---

[48] Titus 2:14

us. We must strive to discern between true and false professions of faith. It is part of the job of the local church to do so.[49]

We aren't the "salvation police," walking around with a magnifying glass and beating people over the head with a Bible. Our responsibility isn't to be Dana Carvey's depiction of the Church Lady. *Well isn't that special.*

This type of judgment is based on *love*—love for the flock and love for the Lord. While pastors bear a particular responsibility to watch over the flock and shepherd the sheep to maturity, *each* member of the local church is also responsible in this endeavor. We watch over one another together.[50]

The local church must not affirm people as believers who are not truly saved.[51] When we haphazardly affirm people as Christians without exercising grace-filled discernment, it is being careless, at best, and sinful, at worst. Grace must permeate our dealings in this matter, but grace does not mean we abandon clear thinking or minimize truth.

This discernment may cause some to label us as "judgmental" in the pejorative sense of the word. We must take intentional precaution to guard against any form of hypocrisy or legalism, but we must also remember that it is the Bible which commands us to exercise discernment about one's profession of faith, though it must be done with love and grace.[52]

[49] Matthew 18:15-20
[50] Galatians 6:1-2, 1 Peter 5:1-5
[51] Malachi 2:17
[52] 1 Cor. 5:12, John 7:24, Matthew 18:15-20

If people wrongly label us as legalistic, so be it, as long as we are humbly seeking to follow what Christ commands of His church. It is *His* standard we must follow, even when people criticize us for doing so.[53] We must hold fast to the totality of His teaching, including the truth that sanctification is not optional to salvation—it is necessary to salvation.

A number of years ago I was teaching on the subject of defining Christians as those who are leaving sin and pursuing holiness. Unexpectedly, a man toward the front of the room interrupted the discussion with a boisterous, "I'd like you to read Matthew 7:1!"

In trepidation, I flipped my pages to the text and began to read, "Judge not that you be not judged. For..." I was immediately cut off with a cold: "*Read it again.*"

Overcoming the initial shock, I regained my composure, obliged the demand, and reread the verse. After this reading, the man proceeded to tell me how this verse means that it doesn't matter how people live, that if they say they are Christians that settles it and we must accept it.

This man, like many others, failed to understand the central truth that though Christians aren't perfect, they are repenters, and a person who lives a perpetually unrepentant lifestyle has no claim to Christ. It is simply not okay for true Christians to pat the unrepentant on the back and act like everything in their life is rosy. The stakes are too high. If they remain in their

---

[53] One day we will answer to Jesus for how we've handled these matters, not anyone else.

deluded state, they will die only to face eternal death in the fiery judgments of hell.

Often, we claim that the problem in our churches is that too many people are immature believers when the real problem is that many we call immature, actually have no life in Christ at all.[54] They aren't growing because they aren't living. Sanctification is missing altogether.

Whereas conversion takes place in a moment in time, sanctification is a lifelong process. Our affections, actions, and attitudes are constantly being worked upon by the Spirit of God through the Word of God, and the fountain of God's grace continually washes over us as we mature in Christ.

The goal isn't to take snapshots of the Christian's walk to search out sin here or there and immediately question the legitimacy of salvation. Rather, the point is to see the big picture in a person's walk with Christ. We rejoice to see that the overall trajectory is one of moving toward Christlikeness. Sometimes that person may even feel plateaued or declining, but the local church can see his or her growth and encourage them to keep running the race.

Christians can and do fall into sin, even grievous sin, but how do they respond when confronted? Is known sin being repented of? Is holiness being pursued? Are the means of grace—such as gathering with the church, partaking of the Lord's Supper, reading the Bible, and prayer—a priority? Perseverance in faith

---

[54] Again, this is if we take Scripture's definition of a Christian seriously. One who is taking up his cross *daily* to follow Jesus. No, this isn't perfect obedience. But it *is* a lifestyle that seeks to conform to Scripture.

means we see ongoing evidence of our walk with Christ. Yes, God *preserves* our faith and I'm grateful that He is the one holding on to me and not the other way around.[55]

As John MacArthur has famously said, "If you could lose your salvation, you would."[56] God *preserves* Christians to the end, but He does so in such a way that believers *persevere* in faith. We fight to the end, and we make it. God will finish what He began in us.[57]

This is why a proper understanding of how salvation works is so important. If we were the ones who chose God apart from any necessity of His grace, then we could also *unchoose* Him at some point in our Christian walk when things get tough for us.

Instead, we can joyfully say that the grace of God chose us, called us, and keeps us to the end in such a way that we actually grow in holiness. And like the good pilgrim, *Christian*, we too will one day cross that river and enter our eternal joy.[58] All true believers will hear Christ say, "*Well done*, my good and faithful servant."[59]

Let's recap. How does salvation work? A person becomes saved when the gospel is proclaimed and the Spirit works through that proclamation in such a way that He moves the sinner from death to life, "turning on the light," so to speak, so that the person sees his or her sin (breaking of God's Law) and

[55] John 10:28

[56] https://twitter.com/tgc/status/574038559662829570?lang=en

[57] Philippians 1:6

[58] See John Bunyan's *Pilgrim's Progress.*

[59] Matthew 25:23

turns from it in repentance, trusting Christ alone in faith as his or her only suitable and all sufficient Savior.

One of the ways we know this is by a person's life—changing from hating God to loving God. In the next chapter, we'll examine a passage of Scripture that demonstrates all we have discussed thus far.

8

From Darkness to Light

"I was lost, but Jesus found me,
Found the sheep that went astray,
Threw His loving arms around me,
Drew me back into His way."
Francis H. Rowley

You must be born again. This truth was a key theme in the preaching of 18th Century Evangelist, George Whitefield (1714 – 1790). It "was a central thrust in his many sermons, namely, the absolute necessity of regeneration in order to gain entrance into the kingdom of God."[2]

Whitefield's unwavering commitment to declaring to sinners their need to be born again, was precisely the type of preaching God used to stir one of the greatest revivals in American history, known as the First Great Awakening. This message stirred the fires of revival in colonial America in such a way that literally

---

[1] From the Hymn *I Will Sing the Wondrous Story.* Words by Francis H. Rowley.

[2] Steven J. Lawson, *The Evangelistic Zeal of George Whitefield* (Crawfordsville, IN: Reformation Trust, 2013), 77.

thousands of people passed from death to life. New England turned upside down—spiritually speaking.

During the years immediately preceding the First Great Awakening, many people claimed to be Christians based on a cultural or ecclesiastical tradition. They professed Christianity merely because their parents made the same confession or because they attended church regularly.

Then burning fires like Whitefield and Jonathan Edwards (1703 – 1758) illuminated the dark landscape of New England by preaching the biblical truth that unless one is born again, he or she will not see the Kingdom of God.[3] These stalwarts of the faith were staunch in their convictions, and clear in their pleading with sinners to flee the wrath to come by coming to Christ in faith.

As a result, God moved upon the hearts of men, women, boys, and girls in a mighty way bringing many sinners from death to life. My hope in such a movement of God today led me to write this book. Join me in praying for revival.

Perhaps this final biblical example will encapsulate everything we've learned so far about the work of salvation. That example comes from the book of Acts. There, the Apostle Paul gives us a gem that clearly illustrates this.

And the Lord said, 'I am Jesus whom you are persecuting. But rise and stand upon your feet, for I have appeared to you for this purpose, to appoint you as a servant and witness to the things in which you have seen me and to those in

[3] John 3:3

which I will appear to you, delivering you from your people and from the Gentiles—to whom I am sending you *to open their eyes, so that they may turn from darkness to light and from the power of Satan to God, that they may receive forgiveness of sins and a place among those who are sanctified by faith in me.'* Therefore, O King Agrippa, I was not disobedient to the heavenly vision, but declared first to those in Damascus, then in Jerusalem and throughout all the region of Judea, and also to the Gentiles, that *they should repent and turn to God, performing deeds in keeping with their repentance* (Acts 26:16-20).

In this passage, Paul recounts his own testimony about how his conversion and his commission from Christ to proclaim the gospel to the nations. In this commission, we receive significant insight into how salvation works.

This isn't some stand-alone passage but one consistent with all we've examined thus far. That's why Scripture is cited throughout this work (and I hope you've been reading the cited passages along the way). With that in mind, let's break down Acts 26:16-20 to see how it connects to the preceding chapters.

Paul's commission was to open the eyes of the Gentiles. First of all, this implies that their eyes were blinded. As we've already discussed, all men are spiritually blind and dead in sin, apart from the grace of God.[4] Isaiah 42:7 says the Messiah's ministry was *to open the eyes that are blind, to bring out the prisoners from the dungeon, from the prison those who sit in darkness.*

---

[4] John 3:19

Spiritual darkness is the place unconverted sinners dwell. It is a place they love. It is where they feel at home. It's not merely that the unconverted *can't* come to the light, but that *they don't want to* come to the light because they hate it.

Yet, it was to these people that Paul was commissioned to proclaim the glories and excellencies of Christ and His blessed gospel. Through this proclamation, sinners' eyes would be opened. This obviously wasn't because of Paul's power but God's power through the gospel.[5]

How comforting to know that Christ not only paid the price for our sins, but also that God doesn't leave us in our spiritual darkness. He sends messengers to proclaim the gospel and He sends His Holy Spirit to open our eyes.

God doesn't paint a masterpiece only to describe it to us. If we are His, He wants us to behold all the richness of this painting, to see every master stroke He made, and to glory in the color and texture of His composition. He opens our eyes to behold it. And again, the means by which this happens is God's power in the proclamation of the gospel.

That's why it's so important to proclaim the gospel to the lost in our communities and to the world. It is through the gospel, and it alone, that the Holy Spirit opens sinners' eyes.

It's not free pizza. It's not dropping Easter Eggs from the sky. It's not a firetruck baptistry. It's not a clever stunt invented by a pastor or ministry leader to entice people to pass through the doors of a church. If we depend on *anything* other than the

[5] Romans 1:16

proclamation of free forgiveness through the finished work of Jesus to be the means by which God opens the eyes of the blind, we are foolish.

It's not baptism, prayer, church attendance, or eating the Lord's Supper that opens one's eyes to the glories of Jesus. It is the power of God in the gospel, period. If we spent more time basking in the glories of the gospel, rather than brainstorming flashy methods to attract people to church, perhaps we would see more people converted.

What do we see happening after this opening of the eyes? Paul says, "that they may *turn from darkness to light...*" Just like Lazarus came out of the tomb, so also sinners come to Christ when their eyes are opened. Until that happens, they not only *can't* come to Christ, but have no *desire* for Him, either.

As Charles Spurgeon (1834 – 1892) wrote, "The sinner's inability lies in his will – it is because he will not that he cannot."[6] Sinners love the darkness and are not willing to come to the light.[7] It's much more comfortable for the sinful soul to willfully slumber in the dreamland of human autonomy than it is to face the truth of the gospel. Little do sinners realize that their slumber is not a place of solace but a cell in which they are imprisoned.

[6] From the Sermon *A Solemn Impeachment of Unbelievers* by Charles Spurgeon. See http://www.spurgeongems.org/vols19-21/chs1207.pdf
[7] John 3:19

But when God turns on the lights, what happens? Paul says they *turn*. Charles Wesley (1707 - 1788) masterfully articulated this biblical truth when he penned:

> Long my imprisoned spirit lay
> Fast bound in sin and nature's night;
> Thine eye diffused a quickening ray,
> I woke, the dungeon flamed with light;
> My chains fell off, my heart was free,
> I rose, went forth, and followed Thee.[8]

God calls us out of darkness and into His marvelous light.[9] He moves us from death to life. Let's recap. This is how salvation works. God opens eyes and sinners come to Christ. He frees us from the slavish captivity of sinful rebellion and awakens us from the faux bed of alternate reality in which we've for too long found a counterfeit comfort.

Awakened, we call out to God on His conditions of mercy, not our own terms. We turn from sin and the power and evils of Satan and, instead, turn to God in faith. This repentance is turning away from the idols of this world and to God in Christ as our only suitable and all sufficient Savior.[10]

Only after this conversion from death to life, do we see deeds come into play. Paul says that converted sinners should be "performing deeds in keeping with their repentance." Works are

[8] *And Can it Be, That I Should Gain.*
[9] 1 Peter 2:9
[10] 1 Thessalonians 1:9

the *result* of salvation, not the means of it.[11] Saving faith is a faith that produces works.[12]

A former pastor of mine used to say, "We don't do good works to get saved. We do them because we are saved."[13] Or, as Thomas Schreiner of the Southern Baptist Theological Seminary writes:

> Justification is by faith alone, but it isn't a faith that is alone, for true faith produces good works. Still, good works are not the ground or cause of salvation; they are the fruit of one's faith. The perfect righteousness of Christ is imputed to believers, so that their righteousness is not inherent but is theirs because they are united to Jesus Christ. At the final judgment God will declare publically what was already the case in the lives of believers, i.e., that they are righteous by faith, and their works will verify (but will not be the foundation of) that declaration."[14]

Or even more succinctly, John W. Tweeddale writes, "Christ is the ground of our salvation, faith is the instrument of our salvation, and works are the fruit of our salvation."[15]

The gospel is *not* our lifestyle. It is not what *we* do. The gospel is *what Christ has done* for us. And yet, this good news

---

[11] Ephesians 2:10, Titus 2:14

[12] James 2:14-26

[13] Thank you, Bro. Gene Tanner.

[14] Thomas Schreiner, *Faith Alone: The Doctrine of Justification* (Grand Rapids: Zondervan, 2015), 78. Schriener also carefully clarifies on page 79 that, "Faith is not our righteousness but an instrument that unites us to Jesus Christ."

[15] *Tabletalk Magazine* from Ligonier Ministries. *What is the Gospel?* (2017). Article by John W. Tweeddale, 23.

does effect true change in us, namely deeds that are in step with repentance which flow out of a transformed heart.

True repentance isn't merely sadness for sin or a desire to escape the consequences of sin. True repentance hates sin and always includes the fruit of sanctification. Repentance and holiness go hand in hand. They are inseparable works of grace. When repentance is real, reformation follows: Reformation in thought, reformation in desires, and reformation in life.

Our affections, actions, and attitudes have been won-drously transformed by the Spirit of God. This involves a love for the people of God and the local church, a desire to follow the ways of God and to obey Scripture, and most importantly it pins all of our hope for salvation and right standing before God on Christ alone.

Many other passages in the Bible teach us about the working of salvation upon the heart of a sinner, but I hope you've seen how this particular passage encapsulates the thesis of this book. To me, it summarizes all we've labored to understand throughout this work.

Paul's mission was to open the eyes of the Gentiles through the proclamation of the gospel in the power of the Holy Spirit so they would turn from darkness to light, receiving forgiveness of sins, and live lives in joyous obedience to Christ the King. This gets to the core of how salvation works.

We used a fictitious *Mike* in Chapter 1 to show how false conversion is so prevalent in our day. Let's now examine a real testimony from a real person for an example of how true conversion takes place.

Charles Haddon Spurgeon's story of passing from death to life on January 6, 1860, is a wonderful example of God's sovereign providence. Let's read it and try to recognize the elements we've covered in this book:

> It was on a wintry Sunday...his school being temporarily closed because of an outbreak of fever, that the 15 year-old Spurgeon found himself in Colchester and on his way to the local Congregational Chapel. But the snow and sleet intensified so that he turned down a side lane called Artillery Street and came to the Primitive Methodist Church. He was thus able incidentally to continue in his determination to visit every congregation in Colchester to find someone who would tell him where he might find relief from the condemnation of the law. His mother had also talked with him positively about this congregation. It is any port in a storm, and so the teenager entered this building for the first time to attend the morning service. There were no more than a dozen or fifteen people present: even the minister had failed to arrive because of the weather. It was the wrong church, the wrong congregation, the wrong weather and the wrong preacher. Into the pulpit climbed a thin-looking man, a shoemaker or tailor, Spurgeon was never to know anything about him. He announced his text as Isaiah 45:22, 'Look unto me, and be ye saved, all the ends of the earth: for I am God and there is none else.'

> Spurgeon says, 'He had not much to say, thank God, for that compelled him to keep on repeating his text, and there was nothing needed – by me, at any rate – except his text. I remember how he said, "My dear friends, this is a very simple text indeed.

It says, 'Look.' Now lookin' don't take a deal of pain. It ain't liftin' your foot or your finger; it is just 'Look!' Well, a man needn't go to college to learn to look. You may be the biggest fool, and yet you can look... A child can look. One who is almost an idiot can look. However weak, or however poor a man may be, he can look. And if he looks the promise is that he shall live." He went on in his broad Essex accent, "Many on ye are lookin' to yourselves. But it's no use lookin' there. You'll never find any comfort in yourselves. Some say look to God, the Father. No, look to Him by-and-by. It is Christ that speaks. I am in the garden in an agony, pouring out my soul unto death; I am on the tree, dying for sinners; look unto Me! I rise again. Look unto me! I ascend into heaven! Look unto me. I am sitting at the Father's right hand. O poor sinner look unto me! Look unto me! Some of ye say, 'We must wait for the Spirit's workin'. You have no business with that just now. Look to Christ. The text says, 'Look unto Me.'

The preacher managed to spin that out for ten minutes and then, running out of anything fresh to say, looked at his congregation and picked on Spurgeon, 'Young man, you look very miserable,' he said. 'Well,' said Spurgeon, 'I did look miserable, but I had not been accustomed to have remarks made from the pulpit about my personal appearance before. However, it was a good blow, struck right home.' The preacher went on, 'and you always will be miserable – miserable in life and miserable in death – if you don't obey my text; but if you obey now, this moment, you will be saved.' And then he shouted at the top of his voice as I think only a Primitive Methodist can, 'Young man, look to Jesus Christ. Look! Look! Look! You have nothing to do but to look and live!' And I did look.

I saw at once the way of salvation. I know not what else he said – I did not take much notice of it – I was so possessed with that one thought. Like as when the brazen serpent was lifted up, the people only looked and were healed, so it was with me. I had been waiting to do fifty things, but when I heard that word, 'Look!' what a charming word it seemed to me.

Oh I could have looked until I could almost have looked my eyes away. There and then the cloud was gone, the darkness had rolled away, and that moment I saw the sun; and I could have risen that instant, and sung with the most enthusiastic of them, of the precious blood of Christ, and the simple faith which alone looks to him. O that somebody had told me this before, 'Trust Christ, and you shall be saved.'[16]

From death to life. Certainly not everyone gets caught in a snowstorm as a catalyst to their salvation, but other than that, Charles Spurgeon's story of salvation is not overly unique. The true gospel was proclaimed (and that not professionally). The Spirit of God moved in his life and Spurgeon trusted Christ alone as his only suitable and all sufficient Savior. As a result, Spurgeon went on to bear much fruit for Christ. Certainly, there have been few Charles Spurgeons in the history of the church in terms of gospel impact, but that aside, all Christian testimonies are similar.

If you've been saved, it's a miraculous story! You who were dead in your sins were brought to life by the power of God in the gospel. You were rebellious, wicked, proud, and sinful, but God's grace knocked you off your high horse. Your cold dead

---

[16]   https://banneroftruth.org/us/resources/articles/2000/the-conversion-of-charles-haddon-spurgeon-january-6-1850/

black heart was brought to life by the sovereign grace of our glorious God.

It may have been in a church service, or in a gospel discussion over fast food, or in a conversation with a passenger while driving down the interstate. Any person who has come to Christ in faith has done so because the gospel has been declared, God has moved effectually, and he or she has responded appropriately to the command to repent and believe, and went on to live a life of following Christ as Lord and Savior. Your eyes were opened and you turned to God in repentance.

What I hope you've seen is that the central focus in conversion is not a ritualistic prayer, but the movement of God upon a sinner by means of the proclamation of the gospel whereby the sinner comes to Christ in saving faith and repentance. That nearness is not a mere turning of the lips but the turning of the heart. This is how salvation works. And in this we joyfully say, "All glory be to God!" Amazing pity, grace unknown, and love beyond degree.[17]

[17] Isaac Watts, *Alas! And Did My Savior Bleed?*

9

Putting It All Together

"The greatest need of the church today is a strategic, full-orbed, robust, biblical grasp of the Gospel of Jesus Christ and its transformative implications."
Dan Phillips[1]

In the late 1940s, my grandfather served in the United States Air Force during the American Occupation of Japan. For a portion of his service there, my grandmother and two aunts had the opportunity to live overseas with him.

Being a young mom living abroad with two preschool daughters, my grandmother got creative one December to help keep her children occupied. She decided to bake Christmas cookies.

Decades before I was born she changed my life forever. You see, these mouthwatering treats turned out to not just be *any* Christmas cookies, but with the help of a special Santa cookie cutter she found overseas, she invented the best cookies ever. Sort of like the guy who accidently created Velcro, my grandmother stumbled upon a wonderful Christmas tradition that has now been in our family for 70 years. What started out

[1] Dan Phillips, *The World Tilting Gospel: Embracing a Biblical Worldview & Hanging on Tight* (Grand Rapids: Kregel, 2011), 19.

as a way to help two little girls stay busy during Christmas turned into one of my all-time favorite family Christmas traditions. Though my grandparents are both gone now, we remember them each Christmas season as we bake these sweet Santa-shaped treats.

Every year Meemaw would spend countless painstaking hours carefully preparing these cookies and mailing them to friends and family. When my siblings and I came along she would patiently work with us to bake them and decorate them with the proper technique. There's a special "Nelson way" these things have to go together.

My wife almost didn't make it into the family for this reason. Before we were married, she came to help us decorate our beloved Santa Cookies and proceeded to pick one up and decorate it like a gingerbread man. *Mistake!*

These cookies require precision—in making the dough, in cooking time, and in frosting methods. If you fail anywhere along the way, you just don't get Meemaw cookies, which are literally the best cookies ever. No one's allowed to mess 'em up!

It's important to understand how things fit together. Whether you're building the Millennium Falcon Lego set with your 9-year old or baking and decorating cookies, understanding the process of how things go together is vital to completing your task successfully. If you don't understand the process correctly, you don't end up with the desired outcome.

Vastly more important is the comprehension of salvation. The fruit of such knowledge is not just so we can have intellectual, theological conversations over coffee. It's not so we can make clever memes for social media. It matters because people matter. We long to see souls brought from death to life. It matters because we want to see our friends, family, and neighbors truly following Jesus.

If we can spend hours perfecting hunting, playing an instrument, practicing sports, or learning to cook, isn't it worth our investment to understand how salvation works? If we fail to understand how things work in salvation, then there is a dangerous tendency to go astray in a number of areas, just like we are witnessing in today's evangelicalism.

So, how does a person become saved? The definition we've been working with is this: *A person is saved when the gospel is proclaimed and the Spirit works through that proclamation in such a way that He moves the sinner from death to life so that the person sees his or her sin (breaking of God's Law) and turns from it in repentance, trusting in Christ alone in faith as his or her only suitable and all sufficient Savior.* We've spent the majority of this book trying to flesh out this definition, grounding it firmly in Scripture and seeing what it looks like in practice.

A correct understanding of the above should sharpen our faithfulness to the one true gospel and to biblical evangelism. It should cause us to joyfully proclaim to the nations, "Look to Christ and be saved!"[2] It should fill us with the wonder of the glory of God in Christ—that Jesus is supreme and infinitely worthy of our adoration, love, and worship. Instead of resorting

[2] Isaiah 45:22

to gimmicks, it should embolden us and encourage us to preach, speak, and share the one true gospel as faithfully and consistently as humanly possible. Trust its power! As Jim Elliff writes:

> What makes the gospel so powerful? It is the reality that Christ lived the perfect life we could not live, that he died on the cross as God's perfect Son to bear the sins of sinning and damned people just like us, and that he rose again to conquer the dominance of sin and death. That reality is powerful because there is nothing else to substitute for it – nothing else that does the job that Christ did before his holy and just Father.[3]

What inexplicably glorious news! The gospel is the power of God unto salvation. Tell a friend, share a tract, preach on the street corner, and watch God work. Tweet, post on Facebook, send a letter, send an email, send a carrier pigeon. Publish the good news among the nations. The King is coming to judge in righteousness but He has offered terms of peace by His life, death, and resurrection. *Repent and believe the gospel.*

Understanding how a person becomes saved causes perseverance in gospel proclamation. Perhaps you're not seeing the fruit you'd like to see, but because you know God delights in bringing sinners from death to life, you keep on preaching. Don't quit. Don't hold back. Your job is to communicate the gospel. The results belong to Him. Keep pointing sinners to Christ and God will save.

---

[3] Jim Elliff, *Pursuing God: A Seeker's Guide* (Kansas City, MO: Christian Communicators Worldwide, 2010), 49.

You won't always see the full fruit of your labors. Sometimes others harvest the seed you planted. However, we can rest in the confidence that God can take the simplest seed sown in a sinner's heart and bring them to salvation. Who knows? Even after we're gone, people may turn to the Lord because of our efforts here on earth. Keep sowing those seeds. Persevere in proclaiming the gospel.

Adoniram Judson (1788 – 1850), one of my favorite missionaries, served in Burma, India for nearly 38 years. His first wife, second wife and several children died while he was serving on the mission field. He also suffered in a Burmese prison for seventeen months under unimaginably harsh conditions. Still, he kept preaching.

It took him six years of gospel preaching before he saw his first convert.[4] By God's grace, he kept preaching, and "when Adoniram Judson died in 1850, there were 7,000 baptized believers, 63 Christian congregations and 163 missionaries in Burma. To this day, over 150 years later, his Burmese Bible translation is still in use."[5]

Judson is an example of a man who trusted God with the results of his preaching. He didn't consider his success in terms of numbers of converts. Instead, he faithfully did what Christ told us to do—preach the word, in season and out. His methods

---

[4]   http://www.christianitytoday.com/history/issues/issue-90/man-who-gave-bible-to-burmese.html

[5]   https://www.christianity.com/church/church-history/church-history-for-kids/adoniram-judson-first-missionary-from-the-united-states-11635044.html

were biblical and because of his perseverance, God brought dramatic results.

> He was a seed that fell into the ground and died. And the fruit God gave is celebrated even in scholarly works like David Barrett's *World Christian Encyclopedia*: 'The largest Christian force in Burma is the Burma Baptist Convention, which owes its origin to the pioneering activity of the American Baptist missionary Adoniram Judson' (David Barrett, ed., World Christian Encyclopedia (New York: Oxford University Press, 1982., 202).[6]

That's the power of God in the gospel. A biblical understanding of how salvation works helps us persevere in proclaiming the good news that God saves sinners through the life, death, and resurrection of Jesus.

This isn't just for pastors and missionaries either. The power of God in the gospel should propel all Christians to have a laser-like, repetitive, and unceasing focus on Christ and His work as we go about our lives sharing His good news. How wonderfully freeing.

A killer testimony isn't necessary to captivate people. You have the gospel. People don't need to know about what happened to you as much as they need to know about what happened to Jesus.

Furthermore, this means we don't have to stay ahead of the church growth curve in order to remain relevant. We have the

[6] From John Piper's sermon, *How Few There Are Who Die So Hard!* (2003). Source: https://www.desiringgod.org/messages/how-few-there-are-who-die-so-hard

most relevant news in all the universe: *Jesus saves.* Keep proclaiming the gospel and see God work for His own eternal glory.

> *Bear the news to every land,*
> *Climb the steeps and cross the waves;*
> *Onward!—'tis our Lord's command; Jesus saves! Jesus saves!*

God still pulls folks out of the miry clay and sets their feet upon the Rock.[8] He is still in the wretch-saving business. You don't need gimmickry to make God great.[9] He doesn't need your creativity. He already *is* great and He delights in the salvation of sinners. Go and tell.

Additionally, this understanding of salvation gives us great comfort as saints and gives all glory to God for His work in bringing us from death to life. God saved me and God will keep me. He loves me and I can be wholly assured that nothing in this world will change that because He bought me with the precious blood of Christ.[10]

God gets 100% of the credit for my salvation from beginning to end. I am not saved because I was smarter, better, or harder working than anyone else. Rather, I am a Christian solely on the basis of God's amazing grace. This is true of all believers. We will spend an eternity as Christians praising our triune God for His grace in salvation. *Soli Deo Gloria* – Glory to God alone.

[7] From the hymn, *Jesus Saves* by Priscilla J. Owens.
[8] Psalm 40:2
[9] Isaiah 40:9b
[10] Romans 8:31-38

Next, this understanding of salvation should drive us to a vibrant prayer life. It's not our cleverness or charisma that wins souls but the work of God in Christ through the Holy Spirit's application. If the Spirit doesn't move, no one gets saved.

Ask Him to move in hearts today! Pray for the kingdom of God to expand.[11] Does not God desire the salvation of sinners even more than you do?[12]

Since, apart from Christ, we can do nothing, we need to pray. Prayer is a means by which God opens opportunities to share the gospel.[13] If we understand how salvation works, we will be people of fervent prayer for God to save the lost.

This understanding of how salvation works should also fill us with steadfast hope. God hasn't quit saving sinners, nor will He as long as this world is turning. God is still saving sinners through the life, death, and resurrection of Jesus Christ for His own eternal glory. When we share the gospel faithfully, and desire to see sinners come to Christ, we align our desires with the Lord's.

True, many may reject the gospel you offer as God leaves them to their own sinful choices. Keep in mind they're not rejecting us, but rejecting God. Whether they respond favorably to the gospel we proclaim depends upon the Lord. Our job is to share the gospel. His job is to bring sinners to Himself.

We know that because He's told us to go make disciples of all nations. So carry the banner of Christ confidently through

[11] Matthew 6:10
[12] 2 Peter 3:9
[13] Colossians 4:3

your neighborhood, in your work place, and to the nations, confident in knowing that God saves. Don't quit, for God is using us to bring His eternal plan to fruition.

The knowledge of how a person gets saved should also drive us to pristine clarity on the true nature of biblical faith and repentance. Too many people think repentance is just feeling bad about sin.

A young man sleeps with his girlfriend Saturday night, feels bad Sunday morning, walks the aisle after the sermon, and goes back to bed with her Sunday night thinking he's repented. But that's not repentance. Repentance turns away from the sin and turns toward obedience to Christ.

If we are genuine believers, we will be sold out to Christ's agenda, not our own. Faith is a gift of God whereby the sinner trusts Christ, believes in Christ, rests in Christ, wants Christ, treasures Christ, and longs to do Christ's bidding as revealed in Scripture.

Jesus had a knack for making sure people understood what they were getting into in salvation.[14] He didn't just say, "affirm the facts about who I am and you're good to go." This isn't because Jesus was attempting to make it harder to follow Him. This is about explaining what it truly means to enter the narrow gate and to walk the hard way.[15]

When we proclaim Christ, we shouldn't mislead people about what life in Him is all about. The Christian life is joyful,

[14] Luke 9:57-58
[15] Matthew 7:13-14

but it is also hard sometimes—denying self, taking up our cross daily, and following Christ wherever He leads us.[16] That's difficult stuff. Yet we do it, not in our own strength but in His.

Our desire to see people come to Christ is about more than another "soul-winning" notch in our belt. We sincerely care for them. If we love God and man we must explain the commitment involved in belonging to Him.

Finally, a healthy understanding of justification and sanctification should help us explain to the sinner what happens when they respond positively to the proclamation of the gospel. God has removed our sins as far as the east is from the west and placed us in perfect standing before Him, clothed in the righteous robes of Jesus.[17]

And, if justification has happened, then sanctification is happening. If sanctification is not happening, then that person is still dead in sin.[18] If someone continually and consistently chooses the way of the world and sin over the things of Christ, we have reason to suspect that their conversion was not genuine.[19]

Christians are not perfect people, but they are repenting people. Thus, a proper understanding of how salvation works

[16] Luke 9:23

[17] Psalm 103:12

[18] It's impossible to be a Christian and not undergo sanctification. It may be happening even if we don't perceive it. It's not always easy to see. But it is always happening over the course of our life.

[19] 1 John 2:15-17

will also help us recover the biblical practice of church discipline.

Church discipline is loving people enough to confront them when they are in sinful error. It is not done to rain judgment over their heads, but more in the hope that they will leave behind any sin in which they've presently strayed and return to the fold. Since Christians are lifelong repenters, it is an expectation and hope of the church that, when confronted with this kind of discipline, members found in a *pattern* of sin will repent and be restored to fellowship.

Sadly, that doesn't always happen. Some people occasionally dig their heels in when confronted and return to their sin with renewed zeal, rejecting the church and its representatives—and thus rejecting Christ. In such a case, we must remove this person from the membership of the local church. Jesus says we are to treat these as unbelievers.[20]

The point here is that understanding how salvation works has an enormous impact on numerous things in the personal life of a Christian and in the corporate aspect of the church. Even when it's difficult, we are still commanded to obey Christ. And I'm grateful the Lord has given us other Christians to aid us in this journey.

One of the most difficult questions for me early in ministry was how to get people to move from death to life. What can we do to move them across the finish line?

[20] Matthew 18:15-17

In my youthful zeal, I employed the Sinner's Prayer to help lost people "close the deal" with God, only to be left saddened a few months or years later when they didn't stay with the Lord. Now I realize I was wrong in my explanation to them of how a person becomes saved. I needed to repent—and I did.

But do you know what? The blood of Jesus is enough to cover that sin too. If you've misrepresented this crucial issue, I invite you to repent as well, and trust that you are forgiven in Christ. Let us go forward together in hopes of correcting any misinformation we've put forth in the past. Our churches will be better for it.

What *can* we do to help them across the finish line, to accept Christ? The plain teaching of Scripture is staring us right in the face: *We* can't do anything but plant the seed—by communicating the gospel in a way lost sinners can understand. *God* must open the heart.[21] *God* must remove the heart of stone and replace it with a heart of flesh.[22]

Practically speaking, this means that I must plead with sinners to come to Christ, but I can't bring them to Christ through any power of my own. I must articulate the glories of Jesus and proclaim His gospel faithfully and call the sinner to repent and believe the good news, but I must *trust God with the results.* After all, salvation belongs to the Lord.[23]

This doesn't mean sinners are passive in coming to Christ. Quite the contrary. They're *eager* to repent and believe the

[21] Acts 16:14
[22] Ezekiel 36:25-27
[23] Jonah 2:9

gospel when God draws them. They've been given eyes to see Jesus.

The truth is they are never going to choose Christ if I treat the gospel like a used car I need to sell. They are only going to choose Christ if God overcomes their rebellion against Him and draws them to Himself by His grace. So, proclaim the gospel faithfully, call sinners to place their trust in Christ, and rest in God to do what only He can do for His own glory.

Understanding how salvation works is a conversation worth having. It is worth discussing. It is worth arguing over, if necessary (in love), so that we can make sure we truly understand *God's* way of converting sinners. We should be able to have these sorts of conversations without getting mad at one another. Souls are at stake. The health of our churches is at stake. Let's make sure we get this right.

May we be wholly confident in the Lord of hosts. No matter the conditions of our country may we seek to serve our worthy King with all our might. May we preach the gospel urgently, love the church fervently, and commit ourselves to the Scriptures relentlessly.

Because at the end of the day, we must remember that what we desire above all else is not a particular system but a *biblical* understanding of how a person moves from death to life. We must, above all, be Bible people.

It ultimately doesn't matter what my personal opinion is, or what yours is, or even sweet Mrs. Edith's. What matters is what the Bible says. It is still our highest authority, not tradition or experience. And it is still wholly sufficient for all things pertaining to life and godliness which includes how a person moves from death to life. Here we stand indeed.

10

Plant, Water, Trust God, Repeat

*"Every saved person this side of heaven owes the gospel to
every lost person this side of hell."*

David Platt[1]

"For three games my son hasn't been able to pitch well!," stated
one of the members of our church as he burst into my office.
Being confronted with such a complaint took me off gaud.
Having recently entered into the ministry, I didn't realize that I
would ever have to face such a criticism. Yet, according to this
man, our church was responsible for his son's poor pitching.

You see, prior to this young man's pitching slump, our youth
pastor had explained how sports can become an idol in our
lives. This brought conviction to this young pitcher. He had
already been under a measure of conviction, which his mother
sought to dismiss by saying: "Honey, you are *already* saved!"
Yet, apparently these words were ineffective in easing the boy's
guilty conscience. And, learning that sports had become an idol
in his life, his conscience became even more burdened. And

begin
[1] David Platt, *Radical: Taking Back Your Faith from the American Dream*
(Colorado Springs: Multnomah Books, 2010), 74.

with uncertainty of his own salvation, it became difficult for him to sleep and to strike out batters at the plate.

For me, it seemed apparent that this young man needed spiritual counsel. His parents, however, did not agree. They were more concerned about his shaken confidence in throwing a baseball across a 17-inch wide pentagon than they were about his eternal security.

I share this story to convey that understanding how salvation works is a big deal. Applying it to real life scenarios is not always easy. What's easy is to simply have people pray a prayer after us, never question it again and then move on. If they turn away at a point in their life we chalk it up as them being backslidden. Though that may be the easiest way to push our agenda on someone else, it is not how to evangelize the lost.

One of the main purposes of this book has been to eliminate that sort of mentality and replace it with a biblical approach. If our desire is for the salvation of the lost, we must do whatever it takes to proclaim the truth in love. Assembly line Christianity is much easier than biblical Christianity. Biblical Christianity is a real war, with real people, real sins, real wrestling, real apostasy, and real souls at stake.

And so, if a person comes to us wanting to be saved, how should we handle it? How do we lead them to Christ?

Understanding how a person gets saved isn't something that belongs only in the theological realm. It's not something better left to "trained professionals." This ought to matter to *all* believers.

Why? Because right theology produces proper methodology, and all Christians are charged with communicating the good news of the gospel to a lost and dying world. Every single one of us is charged with sharing the gospel with those God providentially places in our life.

The church gathers on Sundays but scatters throughout the week. You will reach places every day that your pastor can't access as easily as you can. You have influence over people he wouldn't ever know—perhaps your boss, your coworkers, the librarian you know so well, your neighbor who borrowed your leaf blower, your cousin, Eddie.

The Lord's kind providence means none of those people are in your life by chance. They need to hear the gospel. And so, after sharing the gospel, if a person wants to be saved, what should you do?

This is an especially important question if you're a parent. Is there anything more important to you than your children's salvation? When your child comes to you and asks you how to be a Christian, how will you respond to that life-changing question? That's why understanding this is so important. That's why it's vital that we *all* know what to say when the time comes to share the gospel of Christ.

In chapter one, we discussed a fictitious *Mike* who was led in a prayer at twelve years old at a Vacation Bible School, but never actually became a Christian. Put yourself in the instructor's place at that VBS.

Little 12-year old Mike comes to you with questions about salvation. What do you do? Both in Scripture and history we see the circumstances surrounding conversion happen in a variety of ways.

Spurgeon heard a sermon from a layperson. George Whitefield read a book by Henry Scougal.[2] John Newton recalled Scripture he had memorized as a child. The Philippian jailer was on the brink of committing suicide. But all of these stories, in fact *every* conversion story, is tied to the proclamation of the gospel and a response of faith.

There is no formula. If we were given a formula we would use it wrongly. In fact, we *weren't* given a formula at all, but that didn't stop some people from creating one and then using it wrongly—for instance, telling people to say these words and they are saved, or being baptized, or repeating a prayer.[3] It's not as easy as taking people through the ABC's of becoming a Christian and voila! now they are saved.

It is essential that the facts of the gospel are understood. As the old adage goes, "people need to know they are lost before they can be saved." All persons, even children, who wish to be saved need to understand they have broken God's Holy Law and stand justly condemned before Him. They need to understand their only hope of rescue is the redemption offered in Christ by His life, substitutionary death, and resurrection.

[2] I highly recommend *A Modernize Version of The Life of God In the Soul of Man* by Henry Scougal (Conway, AR: Free Grace Press, 2017).

[3] For more thoughts on the Altar Call and The Sinner's Prayer, see Appendices 1 and 2.

They need to understand that, though salvation is a gift freely given, there will be a cost in following Jesus—that He bids us to take up our cross and follow Him.[4]

Sinners need to recognize that they are called to respond to the gospel, which involves understanding the nature of saving faith and biblical repentance. It is not wise, nor loving, to minimize any of these truths. If a person does not understand any of the above facts, we must be willing to labor with them until they do. In the book of Acts, the Apostles didn't merely proclaim the gospel and call it a day, but were also willing to reason with their hearers, and to teach them what was right.[5]

Don't gloss over the facts of the gospel. We are not the shady used car salesman who gives just enough information to close to deal, while hiding some of the most important facts. Endeavor to help the sinner understand the truths of the gospel without making it appear that we are grilling them for entrance into Harvard.

Sometimes, all of the facts of the gospel *are* understood, at least on a cognitive level. So, what do we do then?

Depending on one's understanding, it may be when a person says they want to be saved that you urge them to call out to God. Or it may be you need to explain the gospel further, showing the reality of God's holiness and the wickedness of our trampling His Holy Law. Or you might need to explain what it means that Jesus died in our place. Or it may mean you need to

[4] Matthew 16:24-26
[5] Acts 17:2, 18:4

give the sinner time to himself, alone with God, to process these truths.

Sometimes we can say too much. Silence isn't always a bad thing. Give people time to consider their status before a holy and righteous God. Maybe they've come to you after they have *already* repented and believed on Christ and need help sorting that out.

Remember, every sinner has a cold, dead heart that stands in need of the sovereign regenerating work of the Holy Spirit before he or she will ever truly embrace Christ. Trust Him to work, even as you faithfully deal with each situation on a case by case basis.

Maybe you need to explain to the person you are talking with what a Christian actually is. Maybe you need to commit to meet with them regularly for the purpose of reading Scripture together, of learning more about this loving Savior. It may be that during one of these meetings you see that God has done a work and they've truly been born again. It is biblical to meet with lost people to work through Scripture.[6] Reason with them from the Word of God.

An endless number of scenarios may occur in the process of conversion. From Lydia to Cornelius. From Paul to Peter. From young Timothy to your own son.

There's no particular formula. Salvation is an individual miracle occurring in the heart of each believer. There are no

---

[6] Acts 17:11

"boring" testimonies because any person who comes to Christ has been brought from death to life.

A person gets to Christ by *coming to Him.* It really is that simple. The sinner, in response to God's work, must turn *to* Christ and *away* from sin.[7] This is not a turning of the lips, but a turning of the heart. Out of the abundance of the heart, the mouth speaks.[8] Faith will manifest itself in calling out to God.

What does this look like? Some similarities may exist—like a jubilance present after conversion that wasn't there before, but this is such an individual experience that we can't draw a perfect picture of it. One may shout in joy, while another softly cries tears of joy.

Calling out to God in faith may be expressed in a variety of ways. The words may not be eloquent, or in Elizabethan English, but they will express to God a humble desire to thank Him for all that Christ is and has done for them. That prayer might not even be audibly spoken, for that matter, but a mere whisper inside the confines of one's new heart, or simply a soft, "God be merciful to me, a sinner."[9]

The words may be said in a variety of ways. And if that person has genuinely been brought from death to life, the words don't matter at all. However, if that sinner is merely going through the motions without engaging the heart, then all the

[7] 1 Thessalonians 1:9
[8] Luke 6:45
[9] Luke 18:13

eloquence in the world will be discarded rubbish in the Lord's ears.

So, what would you tell little Mike? Hopefully, you would explain the gospel and then tell him that the only appropriate response is that he repents and believes. It doesn't matter if you're 12 or 112, no one gets saved apart from repenting of sin and believing the gospel.

Don't put words in Mike's mouth. Articulate the gospel and ask him if he understands. Key open-ended questions are helpful in gaging whether or not he is "getting it."

What is sin? What is repentance? If God were to allow you into heaven, on what basis would He do so? Why did Jesus die on the cross? What is the gospel? How did Christ's death on the cross save anybody?

Again, don't expect seminary level understanding, but based on someone's answers you should be able to assess if they accurately comprehend the gospel. Be willing to discuss, engage, and explain. Be willing to listen with compassion and discernment.

Explain their need to call on Christ for salvation and let them speak on their own. Help them understand by using biblical language like believing, calling, and trusting instead of extra-biblical language such as, "asking Jesus into your heart." This requires you to be well read in the Scriptures. Spend time memorizing, meditating on, and studying the Scriptures, knowing that they are the very words of life to souls wrestling with salvation. Speak Bible to them.

Most importantly, trust God to do His work. The Holy Spirit's got this. Do your part in sharing the gospel and explaining what is required for a person to be saved.

You can pray *for* Mike, but you can't call out to God for him. Only Mike can do that and he will only do that if he understands the gospel. It's okay if you are not around when Mike actually calls on Christ. Sometimes we have such an eager desire to *see* conversion that we want to rush a person into doing *something* so we can feel confident that they "got it."

God doesn't always work that way. Do your part in communicating the message of Christ, and then trust God to work as He wills.

This goes for *any* lost person. Because of their sinful and stony hearts, sinners will only understand the gospel if the Spirit is working, which is something you have no control over. So, share the gospel. Be willing to labor. Strive to be clear. Show them your concern for their soul. Implore them to be reconciled to Jesus.[10] Then concede to the Holy Spirit to do His work.

Whatever you do, don't try to play Holy Spirit in anyone's life. You don't have the power to move anyone from death to life, only God does. You cannot overcome their sinfulness and hardness of heart. Their depravity is so serious, it will take the supernatural power of God for them to become a Christian.

Never manipulate a person into a decision she doesn't understand. Assist her in understanding what it means to count

[10] 2 Corinthians 5:20

the cost. Sometimes in the gospels when people said they wanted to follow Jesus, He actually talked them *out* of it.[11] No, you don't know the hearts of people. The point I'm making is that not everyone who says they want to be a Christian *really* wants to be a Christian.

I'm not saying we should make it *harder* for people to get to Christ, but we should be wary of trying to move people from death to life when only the Holy Spirit can do that. *They* must want Christ. Your job is to show them from Scripture why they need Jesus, entreat them to come to Christ, and trust God with the rest.[12]

If it's apparent that a person doesn't understand the gospel it may be appropriate to discuss this further with him. There may come a time when you need to point him to additional Scripture to read on his own and simply end the conversation. Or you may send him home with a gospel tract or other literature. But you must not exploit him by leading him into a false decision.

I once heard about a church camp pastor who told a group of children to, "Just ask Jesus into your heart, and then worry about the repentance stuff later." What terrible, unbiblical advice! In fact, it's possibly damning to those who heard it.

---

[11] Luke 9:57-62

[12] With all this emphasis on God's work, you may be tempted to wonder why you should bother laboring so hard to help people understand the gospel. There are several reasons. 1.) God works through *means*. He uses us to bring about His purposes. 2.) We see this exact methodology used in Scripture. (See Acts 8:30-35). 3.) We care enough about God's glory and the sinner's serious situation that we are willing to labor intensely.

Stay true to the Word and trust that the Lord is able to save. Scripture really is sufficient for these matters. Don't give up on people. When nothing seems to click and you're thinking the appeal is hopeless, you may then find that God was at work in that sinner's heart the whole time. What a joy to see the lights come on in that person's thinking!

No, you might not be able to pinpoint that it was on March 12, at 12:43 pm, but you can see that God has done a work and that the person has trusted Christ for the forgiveness of sins.

The method I'm advocating might be frustrating to some in a results-based church culture, but it is far more faithful to Scripture than the factory mindset of pushing people through a prayer and "out comes a Christian." We live in a microwave society that demands results now.

This has crept into our churches. The church isn't after *results*. We are after souls for the glory of God. Don't put your effort into "closing the deal" but into being as clear, loving, and honest as you can be about the Christian life and the truths of the gospel.

This takes patience. It takes persistence. It takes faithfulness to Scripture. But it's worth it. It is *worth it!*

Truly understanding how salvation works changes how we deal with sinners in need of salvation. Right theology produces proper methodology. And this methodology is worth it!

It is worth every hour you pray. It is worth every tear that you cry. It is worth every long conversation that you have that may seem to be going nowhere. It is worth night after night discussing the gospel with your children even if nothing seems to be happening. It is so worth it to see the miracle of a sinner coming to faith in Christ.

The alternative is easy believism that results in premature celebration, baptism, and an almost certain walking away from Christianity later on. You do not want to be responsible for misleading anyone in a matter as grave as this one.

It is not my intent to take away from the legitimacy of spontaneous decisions for Christ during a worship service on a Sunday morning. Those do happen, of course. Some are saved the first time they hear the gospel. That's the power of God.

The problem is, it is terribly difficult to discern such conversions during a two-minute response time at the end of a typical Sunday morning sermon. It is more faithful to Scripture to counsel with people after a service. This doesn't mean people can't be saved during the closing hymn! But it does mean that we are prudent to counsel with that person beyond their initial expression of a desire to become a Christian.

Pastors and other leaders might be afraid that telling people they want to talk with them more after the service is over will quench the Spirit. I promise you, it won't. If the Sovereign Holy Spirit of God is at work, He doesn't have to have a guitar riff to keep hold of the sinner.

If you are the pastor, make yourself available after service to counsel with people. Great men of the faith, such as Charles Spurgeon and Martyn Lloyd-Jones, in centuries past, practiced this. They gave up their Sunday afternoons to counsel people because they were concerned about the souls of sinners. May we have this much concern today. It is more important than beating the Methodists to the Mexican restaurant.

If you are a church member, invite unconverted people who attended your service into your home for lunch to discuss what they heard. Even if it inconveniences you to do this and forces you to miss your nap or watching a game on TV, it is so worthwhile to help people understand what it means to follow Christ.

Cultural studies may certainly be helpful in understanding the audience we are preaching to. But please don't buy into the lie that what people really need is self-esteem boosters. People need to hear more than, "Jesus loves you." What they need to hear today is what they've *always* needed: to know that they are sinners, that they need a Savior, that Jesus is that Savior, and until and unless they come to Him in faith, they will justly spend an eternity facing the punishment of their sins.

They need to hear that God's magnificent love for His people motivated Him to design a plan to protect them from hell and enjoy Him for an eternity in heaven. He did this by sending Jesus to be our sin bearer. No matter their age, social standing, economic status, appearance or anything else, whether they realize it now or not, their greatest need is this Savior— Christ, the King.

This was true in A.D. 33 and if the Lord tarries, it'll still be true in A.D. 3033. True, we want to speak in such a way that our audience can understand, but we don't want to speak in such a way that minimizes any aspect of the gospel, for it is through the *gospel* that God draws sinners to Christ.

Finally, don't forget to take the gospel to the streets. Share it with your family, friends, coworkers, and neighbors. Share it with the man on the subway. Share it with the cashier at the gas station. Let's break free from the mindset that lost people are supposed to "come to hear" the gospel. Lost people may never come to us to hear the gospel. That's why Jesus told us to *go*.

Now that you have a better understanding of how salvation works, take the gospel with you. Be ready in season and out to tell people about Christ. You don't have to go to some faraway land to do this—just do it "as you go" in your own walk of life. God may have mercy on the ones you share with and may use your message to bring sinners from death to life.

Let me mention though that we *do* want to see the gospel go to faraway lands. If you believe the truths set forth in this book, you must be willing to fund gospel endeavors both domestic and foreign. Because we trust the power of the gospel, we can be generous in giving our time and money toward exposing all people to the saving message of Jesus Christ.

I've already discussed baptism, but I want to extend one more plea regarding this crucial subject: don't baptize children too early. I do not think there is a one size fits all age for baptizing kids, but I do think there is prudence in waiting. Children are impressionable, and will often say whatever is necessary to please adults. With this in mind, don't be too hasty to admit them to the baptismal waters just because they've said "yes" to the right questions.

Continue meaningful dialogue with them. Look for fruit. We want to see the fruit of the Spirt in someone's life, not merely a modification in behavior.[13] I'm not suggesting children cannot come to Christ. In fact, I think, by God's grace, children can and do come to Christ, sometimes at a young age.

However, I have seen too many kids respond to an Altar Call, say a prayer and immediately be baptized, only to later abandon their beliefs. Providentially, some eventually come to Christ in genuine faith later in life, and are then genuinely baptized.[14]

Justin Peters warns us:

It should be obvious to even the casual observer that most of the children being baptized in evangelical churches do not grow up to lead lives commensurate with their childhood professions of faith. Some may maintain a casual relationship with 'Christianity' and church but their lives are not markedly different form their unsaved peers.[15]

This is not to scare us, but to exhort us toward biblical prudence.

---

[13] Galatians 5:22

[14] Baptists don't "re-baptize". At least they shouldn't! What Baptists seek to do is actually *baptize*. That is why we do not recognize false baptisms as legitimate baptisms. These include "infant baptism" and other modes of baptism, like sprinkling.

[15] Justin Peters, *Do Not Hinder Them: A Biblical Examination of Childhood Conversion* (Lavergne, TN: Justin Peters Ministries, 2017), 66. I know these are pointed words from Justin, but consider how many children are baptized every year versus the continual downgrade of our society as a whole. If all these children were truly converted, why does society as a whole continue to grow in its hatred toward God? (See *Do Not Hinder Them*, 57).

If a child says to you that she is trusting Christ then please encourage her in that. Continue pointing her to Jesus and walking with her in the Scriptures. Labor to show the child not only the gospel but also the spiritual characteristics of one who is truly trusting Christ.

It doesn't hurt to wait until the members of your local church are confident that you are baptizing a true believer in Christ. It's worth the due diligence to get this right even if it means giving up a certificate from your denomination for "most baptisms in a year." It's worth the due diligence with people of all ages, but children are especially impressionable and easy targets for increased baptismal numbers. Do not play games with their souls.

These are things we must clearly think through in any era, but particularly in one in which we see so many claiming the name of Christ but having no serious love or desire to follow Him. May we see an awakening in our day of gospel fidelity so that the Name of our Great King is extolled among the nations. May our preaching expressly communicate to sinners the need to be born again by the Spirit of God.

May we recover the necessity of saving faith and repentance. May we give all glory to God for salvation. May we see a great recovery of biblical methodology in our day and as a result see an increase in faithful evangelism. May the Lord again bring reformation.

We want the same thing—to see a bountiful harvest of souls come into the Kingdom. He is mighty to save! May we see this happen in our churches to the glory of God alone.

A Closing Appeal

While my primary focus has been on writing to believers, I recognize that unbelievers may also read this book. Maybe this is the first time you've read these truths. Or maybe you're like *Mike* in chapter 1, trusting a false hope. I'd like to conclude by briefly addressing those who haven't yet turned to Christ in true faith and repentance.

Perhaps you realize you've been trying to be a moral person, but you don't really have a love for Christ in your heart. You aren't concerned about holiness. You don't really care much for the people of God. You have no real interest in reading Scripture and laboring to understand it.

Would you take a moment to consider the gravity of your situation? The sobering reality is *not* what people might think of you if you admit that you're not really saved. The sobering reality is that if you continue in this current state and die, you will spend an eternity in hell because you refused to bow the knee to Christ.

I'm not asking if you repeated a prayer, signed a Bible, or raised your hand at the proper moment when cued by an evangelistic speaker. I'm asking, *are you a true believer?* And if you say you're not, why would you continue in that state?

Repent and believe the gospel this instant! Call out to God for His mercy in Christ and ask Him to save your soul from the impending judgment rightly due you. Don't give lip service to God only to live your life according to your own desires and standards. That is the worst kind of deceit—not only toward others, but toward yourself.

Call out to Christ for salvation. Maybe you're thinking, "I don't know if God is working in me. How can I call out to Him?" That is not your job. You are not told to discern the mysterious actions of the Spirit of God. Sir or Ma'am, you are commanded by the God of heaven to repent and believe the gospel. Do so now!

Ask the Lord to open your eyes and help your unbelief that you might have the faith necessary to lay hold of the promises of Christ. Lay down your rebellion against God. See your sin as the filth and ungodliness it is.

Turn *from* your sin and turn *to* our sin-bearing substitute, Jesus Christ. Believe the gospel. See Christ alone as your only suitable and all sufficient Savior.

Christ receives sinful people. In fact, it's the only type of people He receives. To the hypocrite, harlot, or homosexual, there is hope in Christ. To the self-righteous and self-reliant, there is hope in Christ. To the broken, bound, and battered, there is hope in Christ. There is hope in Christ for any who will have Him in faith.

Leave your life of sin, shame, and sorrow and flee to the Fountain of Life. The Blood of Christ is enough to cleanse any sinner who comes to Him in faith. *Any* sinner.

Why not you, sir? Why not now, ma'am? Today is the day of salvation.[16] This is not a decision you should delay. None of us are guaranteed one more hour on this earth. You may not have another opportunity. Leave the darkness and come to the light. Leave death and come to life. You'll never regret it as long as you live.

---

[16] 2 Corinthians 6:2

Afterword

Thank you for reading this book. I hope it has clarified and sharpened your convictions about how salvation works. It is my hope that this will be a continuing conversation amongst faithful Christian denominations as we seek to see the banner of Christ lifted high in our places of service and areas of influence.

Your mission now is to put these things into practice.

If you are a pastor, your first step may need to continue to learn and grow in your own knowledge of the Bible. The more you understand, the clearer you'll teach the flock God has given you. Isn't that your goal?

If you are not a pastor or in a position of leadership you can pray for those who are. You can speak with your pastor and express to him your concerns and convictions. You may find that your visit will encourage him.

This sort of work isn't meant to be read and then tucked away somewhere in the files of your memory. This is meant to be *applied*. As we seek to fulfill the Great Commission, it is imperative that we understand the truth contained in this book. Let's take this information, apply it, and see people throughout the world truly changed by the power of the gospel. Share His gospel today and trust Him to do the work. Be willing to work patiently and lovingly with others.

Most of all, if you belong to Christ, give thanks to God and praise Him—for He has brought you *from death to life!*

If you'd like to go through this book with someone else, I have written a 9-week small group curriculum in .pdf format, which you may request for free of charge by emailing me at allennelson4@yahoo.com.

Appendix 1

The Sinner's Prayer

Many true believers repeated this or some other prayer at the time of their conversions. I am not saying that if you came to Christ and prayed this prayer, you are not saved. I can't count how many times I've prayed it. I'm saying that people cannot find assurance in Christ based merely on repeating this Sinner's Prayer. Some may have spoken these words who were not true believers. Let me make myself crystal clear. *There is no saving power in the Sinner's Prayer.*

1. The Sinner's Prayer Is Not in the Bible

Check your concordance for the term, "Sinner's Prayer," and you'll come up empty. It is not found in one single verse in Scripture. In the Bible, those who come to Christ are never asked to pray a formula prayer. This should be quite a convincing case against it. Oh, but the Bible doesn't say we *can't* use a formulaic prayer, does it? First of all, that's an argument from silence. Secondly, if the Sinner's Prayer was so vital to someone being saved, why is it not in one place in Scripture? And thirdly, can we not at least agree that we can come into serious error when we begin to want to add things to Scripture that aren't there?

2. The Sinner's Prayer Is an Evangelical Hoop

We rightly reject Roman Catholicism's system of justification by faith *and* works. And yet, some Christian pastors use the Sinner's Prayer as a means of obligating God to save us. It's the hoop we require sinners to jump through in order to get to Christ. We might not articulate it that way, but when we present the gospel and then tell people to pray after us and mean it, that's exactly what we are communicating.[1] "Go through this prayer to get to Christ." And that's just wrong.

3. The Sinner's Prayer Comes from a Desire to "Close the Deal"

We all want to see results. I get that. There is no greater joy besides our own salvation than seeing someone else come to Christ. What a blessing! But it's not up to us to close the deal. We cannot play Holy Spirit. Instead, we must trust Him to work in the heart of sinners and to open their eyes to the truth. Salvation is not some kind of deal we can close if we're sharp enough to bring it off. That mentality often leads to complicating matters even worse and, many times, produces counterfeit Christians.

4. The Sinner's Prayer Comes from a Misunderstanding of Conversion

Sinners are saved by grace through faith. No one is saved without repentance from sin and faith in Christ. A Sinner's

---

[1] In fact, that's what creates confusion over conversion and the Sinner's Prayer. People are always wondering if they "meant it enough."

Prayer may be a kind of expression of that faith in Christ, but the prayer itself does not equal saving faith and repentance.

In other words, you don't conjure up faith via prayer. Instead, sinners calling on God for salvation should express what is in their hearts.

Yeah, but what if they can't express it? Remember, they're new at this. They may not put it as eloquently as we could, but they should be encouraged to pray in their own words.

Yeah, but what if they don't understand it? That's a vital clue that something is amiss. What about the ones who thank God for their parents, and ask for Grandma Pearl to get better, and to help them in school? What if there's absolutely no mention of repentance and profession of faith?

What they pray is a clue as to their understanding and devotion to Christ. If there's no mention of these things, it should tell us more teaching is needed. I would not pretend these have found God. I'd tell them I was encouraged by their prayer, and that we would continue to talk together about Christ. That's all.

If I led them in a prayer they repeated after me, what good would that do if they don't truly understand the gospel? So should I send them out as though they were saved when, in reality, they have no clue what that means?

I confess that in my desire to see people saved, I've been guilty of having them repeat a prayer only to later see that they were never truly converted. I am trying to help you avoid that. Let us focus on being biblical.

Must sinners call on Christ to be saved? Absolutely. But that cry must extend from a penitent heart, not force-fed by an evangelist.

One of the most atrocious pieces I've ever read about this comes from C.S. Lovett's, *How to Be a Successful Soul Winner.* In this book, Lovett tells his readers how to "press for a decision." Read Lovett's own words about how he says you can move a person from death to life:

> You have just said to your prospect...'Jesus is waiting to come into your heart. Will you open the door? Will you let Him come in?' He makes no reply. Great forces are at work inside him. His soul is a battlefield. The Holy Spirit and Satan want his decision. You wish you could jump into his heart and help him, but you can't. So you do the one thing you can do...press him to make a decision...Lay your hand on his shoulder (or arm if a man is dealing with a woman) and with a semi-commanding voice say 'Bow your head with me.' Do not look at him when you say this. He won't act if you do. Instead, bow your head first. The sight of your bowed head, the authority in your voice, the touch of your hand on his shoulder and the witness of the Spirit combine to exert terrific pressure...'Follow me, if you will, and we'll pray together.' 'Dear Lord Jesus – I confess that I am a sinner – and I here and now open the door of my heart – I invite you to come in – I now put my trust in you as my personal Savior. Amen."[2]

<hr>

[2] C.S. Lovett, *How to be a Successful Soul Winner* (Roeland Park, KS: SOS, 1996), 47-48.

Is that really it? I mean, if we could just lay our hands on a person's shoulder and have a little more commanding voice, I mean not *too* commanding but at least *semi*-commanding, we would see more people brought from death to life?

You would almost think such a description was a sick parody, appalling to any person who truly followed Christ our King. But sadly, it is a real book written to try to explain how to win more souls for Jesus.

Even more depressing is that many churches over the last several decades have employed tactics like this, either maliciously or unknowingly, in order to see more people "saved." Instead, they've only increased the zombie horde currently plaguing the modern church. Words are just words if they don't flow from a changed heart. It's about crying out to God from a heart that truly understands our condition before Him. It's about acknowledging that Christ alone is our only hope of salvation.

Consider this example: A husband cheats on his wife. He doesn't know what to do so he goes to his pastor. The pastor says, "Do you know what you did is wrong?" "Yes." "Ok, come with me."

So the pastor and the husband drive over to the husband's home. The pastor goes to the door and tells the husband, "When your wife opens the door, you just repeat after me, and really mean it." The wife opens the door and finds the two men standing there. She doesn't know what to expect, but she is hopeful.

Then the pastor begins:

"Dear wife."

"*Dear wife.*"

"I admit that I am an adulterer."

"*I admit that I am adulterer.*"

"I believe that you are my true wife."

"*I believe that you are my true wife.*"

"Please forgive me and accept me back into the house."

"*Please forgive me and accept me back into the house.*"

The problem with this scenario is not merely that it wouldn't *work*—not in a million years. The problem is the husband might really *mean* every single word he said and still not be repentant. This sort of rhetoric has been employed by pastors, evangelists, VBS workers, Sunday School teachers, church camp preachers, and denominational workers for decades.

I confess to you that I've been guilty of this, too. About a year ago I shared the gospel with a man who had once been in my youth group during my youth ministry days. His response to me was, "I'm already a Christian because you already saved me."

I was broken. Today, we are reaping what we've sown. Our own faulty methodology has led us to where we are now.

My plea for us is that we would stop leading people to come to Christ through a "repeat after me" prayer. Instead, let's share the gospel and call them to repentance and faith. If we feel they understand the message then it's perfectly fine to suggest some things they might pray, but don't have them repeat after you.

I will also say this: It can sometimes be best to clearly explain the gospel, call a person to repentance and faith, and then leave him alone with God. Don't convince them that because they prayed that prayer they are now a Christian—no matter what. No. If they never exhibit the fruit of faith, they were never a believer. What needs to take place for a person to be a Christian is to be born again. Sadly, many have said the Sinner's Prayer but have never been regenerated by the Holy Spirit.

What if you've said that prayer? I've probably said the prayer about 1,000 times growing up! But what we need to understand is that it's not the prayer that saves, but faith alone in Christ alone. If you are holding on to a prayer for your assurance in Christ, even though your life has been an abomination to Him, you need to repent and believe the gospel.[3] It's not whether or not you said the prayer *sincerely* but whether or not you trusted Christ as your only suitable and all sufficient Savior.

---

[3] See Psalm 9:10 for example. The Lord does not forsake those who *seek* Him, as in a continual seeking.

Appendix 2

Acts 2 is Not an Altar Call

The Sinner's Prayer and the Altar Call go hand in hand in our day. I define the Altar Call as an intentional act from the preacher to coerce people to come forward at the end of the service in order to make a decision for Christ. It is one thing to extend an invitation for people to come forward if they have questions, but it's quite another to either emotionally bully, or manipulate hearers to come forward so that the "altars will be full."

Like the Sinner's Prayer, we don't see Altar Calls in Scripture. Jesus didn't issue one after the Sermon on the Mount. We don't see the Apostles incorporating it anywhere in the Epistles, or instructing the church on how to conduct one. But this doesn't stop people from trying to build a case for incorporating them.

In discussing Altar Calls one time, I had a brother tell me: "I fail to see how an Altar Call is in itself substantially different than what happened at Pentecost." It's not overly surprising that someone would say this as I've heard prominent denominational leaders express similar opinions.[1]

Well, then, *was* Acts 2 an *Altar Call*? I don't think one can really build such a case. Here are some very important differences:

1. No Invitation to Come Forward

No one was invited or commanded to come up front. They weren't asked to close their eyes and lift their hands.

They *were* commanded to repent and believe the gospel. Because of our culture, I think we actually see people in Acts 2 "coming forward." I've heard men preach on Acts 2 who actually seem to think that's how it went down. This is a misunderstanding of not only the situation of Peter's preaching but also the point of the text, as well.

2. No Music was Played

There was no invitation hymn in Acts 2. There was not one more verse and there was certainly no low lighting. But for the past almost two hundred years, churches have utilized anything—music, lighting, dry ice, etc.--as a way of "setting the mood." We see none of that in biblical days.

---

[1] It should be noted that an 'altar' is a place where sacrifices are made. Our sacrifice has already been made in Christ. In response, Paul calls us to be a *living* sacrifice, which has nothing to do with going to a 'physical' altar anymore.

3. The Holy Spirit Moved on the Hearers, Not Peter's Manipulation[2]

This is something I've labored to show you. God moves first upon the hearers of the gospel. Then, in this scenario, it's the hearers who are actually the ones who initiate the response to the sermon, not Peter.

They cried out, "What must we do?" It would be simultaneously startling and amazing if someone stood up during one of my sermons and cried out, "What must I do to be saved?" Let's just say that hasn't happened yet.

Too often during an Altar Call, people are asked to make a decision for the sake of making a decision or even driving up an evangelist's "numbers." But in Acts 2, no decision had to be called for. These people were convicted by the Holy Spirit.

4. No One was Asked to Recite a Prayer

This is the end game of Altar Calls. Get the sinner to recite a prayer and then tell them that if they really meant it, they are saved. That's not anywhere close to Acts 2 methodology. Peter commands his hearers to repent and believe the gospel.

Furthermore, he testifies to God's prerogative and sovereignty in salvation saying that "promise is for you and for your children and for all who are far off, everyone whom the Lord our God calls to himself."[3] The gospel was preached, the

[2] Acts 2:37
[3] Acts 2:39

hearers were told what to do, and it was left to them and God. Peter simultaneously calls the hearers to repent while letting them know that it was God who called them. Again, we can't force them to come to Christ. That's the Lord's work in the sinner. So, Peter didn't have anyone repeat after him. Rather he exhorted his hearers to repent and be baptized, an evidence of true saving faith.[4]

Acts 2 is most assuredly not a proof text for Altar Calls. However, it is an amazingly beautiful demonstration of the power of God in the gospel and His willingness to save sinners! Let us rest in that.

Let us also see that Acts 2 shows us that the gospel demands an immediate response. Therefore, let's proclaim the gospel from the rooftops and compel all men without distinction to come to Christ in repentance and faith, *now*. Let us extol the mercies of God in Christ. We must share both the glories of the gospel and the reality of the wrath that remains if sinners refuse to bow the knee to King Jesus. Trust in the work of God in the hearts of sinners, not in our ability to extend an Altar Call.

Again, don't hear me saying that having an open-door policy at the end of a service where people know they can come forward and speak with the pastor or other church leaders during a closing hymn is the same thing as an Altar Call. What I mean when I say "Altar Call mentality" are those who use manipulation in order to achieve results.

[4] Acts 2:38

In God's grace, many people have been converted under such a scheme. But so many more have been falsely led astray. This is why I am appealing to us to drop the Altar Call mentality from our services.

Appendix 3

Putting "Baptist"
Back in Your Church

Recovering a right understanding of how salvation works is crucial to what it means to be a Baptist. Honestly, it really doesn't matter that much to me if you don't have that word in the title of your particular church. I just want to know if the ideology of what it means to be Baptist (which, as a Southern Baptist, I see as synonymous with biblical) is actually instilled in your local church.

One of the crucial marks of what it means to be Baptist is that we believe the local church, so far as we are able to discern, is made up of regenerate members, i.e. people who have passed from death to life. Historically, Baptists have believed in regenerate church membership.

That's another reason why understanding how a person is saved is so crucial. And why it has such practical implications for our churches. I don't want to oversimplify the issue, but in many Baptist churches today, it's very easy to get in, so to speak, and very hard to get out.

For example, any 4-year old who can say yes to the right questions can get baptized in many churches. And that same 4-year old can grow up, live with three different girls, become an alcoholic, not attend any service for five decades, die, and still have his obituary read, "Member of First Baptist Church."

See how easy it is to get in? Well, perhaps we should be a bit more discerning about who remains on our rolls, once they get in. Shouldn't we make sure our membership is made up of those who are truly saved? Then shouldn't we follow reasonable rules of accountability with our members—even if that means practicing the biblical requirement of church discipline?

We need to carefully review our membership rolls, and make sure the people on them actually attend our church. And we must do this for the sake of God's holiness.

Here are three ways to do this:

1. Baptism

I mentioned the example of the 4-year old boy above. In the Southern Baptist Convention "the preschool age group saw a 96 percent increase [in baptisms] from 1974 to 2010".[1] Thankfully, that trend tapered off a little from 2005-2010, but I still think it's a major issue. Can 4-year olds be born again? Well, they are just as dead in their trespasses and sins as a 94-year old. It takes the same sovereign regenerating work of the Holy Spirit in either case.

---

[1] http://www.christianitytoday.com/ct/2014/june-web-only/sbc-pre school-baptisms-under-age-6-southern-baptists.html

But, how do we discern whether or not a 4-year old is really a believer? Are we supposed to simply take their word for it? And then baptize them as quickly as possible?

This is what a lot of churches do. It's like it's the one unpardonable sin in the church to question the validity of someone's profession of faith. Yet, Jesus gave to the local church the keys to the Kingdom.[2] Not that we should mimic everything in the few centuries after the closing of the New Testament canon, but some churches in that era would catechize people up to three years before admitting them to the baptismal waters.

Why? Because they wanted to make sure the church consisted of regenerate members. It's biblical to do so.

I don't mean that we go beyond Scripture to make people jump through hoops that Jesus never intended for the church. But, I believe I've demonstrated by now that I think it is imperative we stop letting every person that walks down an aisle and says they are a Christian to enter the baptistery the next week, especially in a culture like ours where what it means to be a Christian has been watered down (no baptistery pun intended) the last few decades.

We need to recover the biblical teaching of conversion and then make that connection with baptism. Seriously, let's do all we can to ensure that those we baptize are indeed true believers. That's not an unreasonable goal.

I'm not saying every church must have a membership class, although that can be a helpful and viable option. I am saying

[2] Matthew 16:19

each person who wants to join the church must have sufficient counsel with the pastors of the church to ensure (as best they can) that he or she genuinely professes faith in Christ. This counsel requires spending time with the person—maybe an hour, or an evening or three weeks, if that's what it takes to make sure he or she understands the gospel and possesses a genuine desire to follow Christ in obedience through baptism.

Folks can say all the right words and still be unconverted. No, they don't have to pass a written test before we baptize them. But it wouldn't hurt for us to be more careful about this on the front end, so that we don't have people on our rolls who don't really belong there.

2. Covenant

True Baptists think of church membership as a covenantal relationship, and for centuries have expressed this in formal written covenants for the church. Covenants are not meant to exceed the bounds of Scripture. Instead, they are meant to clearly define what membership in the local church is to "look like," and to define expectations for church members.

In some Baptist churches a Church Covenant hangs on the wall and that's it. In others, the Church Covenant is missing altogether. However, it must be stated that a covenant exists in all churches.

Sadly, many of those Church Covenants aren't healthy or even spiritually accurate. They are nothing more than the informal agreement that, "membership here means you get voted in by the church and try to come when you can but there really won't be any accountability from us to you or for you to us." Of course, that's not actually written down anywhere—it's just implied.

In a truly Baptistic church, the idea is not "will we have a covenant or not" but "will we have a biblically accurate Church Covenant or not?" While it might not be necessary to write down such a covenant, I think doing so can be helpful.

Covenants show what sort of lives are expected of the members of the church. They define what the church's understanding of holiness is. They express the church's expectations regarding accountability—both to one another and to the leadership of the church.

But wait! Isn't that already in the Bible? Yes, it is. But a Church Covenant sets down the parameters of how the local church interprets particular aspects of the Bible's teaching. Here is a copy of our Church Covenant at Perryville Second Baptist:

> Having been led as we believe by the Spirit of God to receive the Lord Jesus Christ as our Lord, Savior, and Supreme Treasure, and, on the profession of our faith, having been baptized in the name of the Father, and of the Son, and of the Holy Spirit, we do now in the presence of God and this assembly most solemnly and joyfully enter into covenant with one another as one body in Christ.
>
> We engage, therefore, by the aid of the Holy Spirit to walk together in Christian love; to strive for the advancement of this church in knowledge, holiness, and comfort; to promote its prosperity and spirituality; to sustain its worship, ordinances, doctrines, and discipline; to welcome, and test

biblically, instruction from the Scriptures seeking to grow toward biblical unity in the truth; to contribute cheerfully and regularly, as God has prospered us, toward its expenses, for the support of a faithful and evangelical ministry among us, the relief of the poor and the spread of the gospel through the world.

We also engage to maintain family and personal devotions; to study diligently the word of God; to religiously educate our children; to see the salvation of our kindred and acquaintances; to walk circumspectly in the world; to be just in our dealings, faithful in our engagements, and exemplary in our deportment, to avoid all tattling, backbiting and excessive anger; to seek God's help in abstaining from all drugs, food, drink, and practices which bring unwarranted harm to the body or jeopardize our own or another's faith.

We further engage to watch over one another in brotherly love; to remember one another in prayer; to exhort and encourage each other unto every good word and work; to guard each other's reputation, not needlessly exposing the infirmities of others; to participate in each other's joys; to aid one another in sickness and distress; to cultivate Christian sympathy in feeling and Christian courtesy in speech; to be slow to take offense, but always ready for reconciliation and mindful of the rules of our Savior to secure it without delay; to seek to live to the glory of God, who hath called us out of darkness into His marvelous light.

We moreover engage that when we remove from this place we will as soon as possible unite with some other church where we can carry out the spirit of this covenant and the principles of God's word.

When a person wants to join our church, one of the things I do is make sure they get a copy of our Church Covenant so they can see that we place high importance on church membership and want to be careful that no misunder-standings occur—about doctrine or expectations. We want church membership to *mean* something.

Of course, when you have people desiring to join your church and you walk through a Church Covenant with them, they may balk. But it comes back to what we think the church is to be. And if the local church is to be comprised of regenerate members, we should expect them to act accordingly.

3. Discipline

In one sense, discipline ought to be happening all the time in the church. This formative discipline takes place in the regular teaching ministry of the church. To maintain the integrity of our church membership, it's important to recover *corrective* church discipline.

Current Southern Baptist Church membership hovers just above fifteen million today. It's hard to say how many actually are in church every Sunday, but it's often cited as somewhere around six million.

Gathering with the local church is Christianity 101. Hershael York writes, "The easiest act of obedience for a Christian is gathering with the church for worship on Sunday. It only requires that you get up, get dressed, and get there."[3]

It's appalling that so many people are listed on a church roll somewhere but not actually attending. This illustrates one of the reasons a Church Covenant can be so helpful. The covenant should state (rightfully and biblically) that members are expected to regularly gather.

Of course, if Jane Doe misses a week this doesn't mean you kick her out. But it does mean her absence is noted, and perhaps it would be beneficial to check on her.

Using this example, let's identify what it would look like to biblically practice church discipline. If Miss Doe is persistently absent (and it's not for health or other providential hindrance), she should be lovingly reminded that she is breaking covenant with the church and being disobedient to Scripture.

If she persists in this pattern of absence, the one who spoke to her about this should take two or three others to encourage her to repent and come back into fellowship with the church. If she refuses to listen to them it should be told to the church. And if she refuses to listen to the church, she should be treated as a pagan and removed from the church rolls.[4]

This is not done to punish her, but in the desire that such pressure (gentle at first and more insistent as it goes on) may be used by the Holy Spirit to convict her and bring her back into the fold. Many times, this procedure does just that.

[3] https://twitter.com/hershaelyork/status/934743300485140481
[4] Matthew 18:15-17

Sadly, some do not respond to the pleadings of the church. When they go against what they have *covenanted* to do (see point #2), it is time for church discipline. This also helps to ensure the purity of the church and becomes a demonstration of how the gospel transforms a group of individuals into the likeness of Christ *together.* We need to be careful with church discipline and practice it according to how it is laid out for us in Scripture. It has been abused in the past.

However, the troubling issue in our churches isn't that church discipline is being abused but that's it's completely absent! Some may think this practice is mean and outdated, but in the context of the Bible, it is clear that this is to preserve the integrity of the church and lovingly snatch our members from the fire, when needed. This restoration is God's method for returning the straying lambs to the fold.

Yet, we must be clear and bold. It is not a disgrace to remove someone on our rolls—but it *is* a disgrace *not* to do it where it is needed.

Baptists don't advocate for a sinless church. However, we do advocate for a regenerate church. The expectation of regenerate people is that they live a lifestyle of repentance. Believers still sin. But when they are confronted with sin, the expectation is that of repentance.

Some churches don't practice corrective church discipline because they don't want to come across as unloving. The irony is, not to warn people of sin is the epitome of being unloving. If more local Baptist churches resolved to be serious about church discipline it would reinforce our membership rolls—not destroy them.

It would also be a great benefit to churches, individual believers, and the Kingdom at large. No person who has his or her name on your church roll is guaranteed to keep that name there no matter what until they die. As I said above, membership should mean something.

However, the issue is more sobering than that. Many who have their name on a church roll do not have it in the Lamb's Book of Life. This is why it's so important to recover a regenerate church membership.

When our church votes someone in as a member, we are saying, "Yes! As far as we can tell, you are a believer and will be considered as such." What a travesty that, on the Day of Judgment, so many will look at their respective churches and say, "I thought you said I was a Christian!" You see, some believe church membership is what qualifies them for heaven. It's up to us to teach our flock otherwise—that the *only* qualification for heaven is the blood of Christ and without that, there *is* no salvation.